INTRODUCTION
TO THE
POEM

INTRODUCTION TO THE POEM

Third Edition

ROBERT W. BOYNTON

MAYNARD MACK

BOYNTON/COOK PUBLISHERS
HEINEMANN
PORTSMOUTH, NH

Boynton/Cook Publishers Inc.
A subsidiary of Reed Elsevier Inc.
361 Hanover Street   Portsmouth, NH   03801-3912
Offices and agents throughout the world

Library of Congress Cataloging-in-Publication Data

Boynton, Robert W.
   Introduction to the poem.

   Includes index.
   1. Poetics. 2. American poetry. 3. English poetry.
I. Mack, Maynard, 1909–   . II. Title.
PN1042.B69 1985   808.1   85-13297
ISBN 0-86709-143-6

Printed in the United States of America

99 98 97   14

ACKNOWLEDGMENTS

The authors wish to thank the proprietors for permission to quote copy-
righted works, as follows:

W. H. AUDEN. "As I Walked Out One Evening," "Musée des Beaux Arts," "In Memory
of W. B. Yeats": Copyright 1940 by W. H. Auden. "O Where Are You Going?":
Copyright 1934 and renewed 1961, by W. H. Auden.   These selections are
reprinted from *The Collected Poetry of W. H. Auden,* by permission of Random
House, Inc.

GEORGE BARKER. "To My Mother": Copyright © 1957, 1962 and 1965 by George
Granville Barker. From *Collected Poems 1930 to 1965.* Reprinted by permission of
October House Inc. and Faber and Faber Limited.

HILAIRE BELLOC. "Lines for a Christmas Card": Reprinted by permission of
A. D. Peters & Co.

JOHN BETJEMAN. "In Westminster Abbey": Reprinted from John Betjeman's *Collected Poems* by permission of John Murray (Publishers) Ltd.

SANDRA BOYNTON. "You Are You": Reprinted by permission of the artist.

PREFACE

This third edition of *Introduction to the Poem* retains the basic structure of the first two editions and almost all of the poems that are in the second. We've added a number of poems throughout the book and have expanded the general Introduction. We think the additions add immeasurably to the book's value.

Our aim in this introduction, as in the earlier editions, is to suggest ways of approaching poetry that will remove the bewilderment many people feel about it. We readily admit that often a poem doesn't make immediate total sense, the way a straightforward paragraph like this one does. But a poem makes immediate rhythmic sense if it's read aloud, and the other kind of sense we call "meaning" will come with increasing pleasure if the right approaches are made—if, basically, a reader respects his or her native wit and lets the poem do its work (and if, of course, teachers encourage such response). The approach here helps clarify what a poem is and does, and how a good reader reenacts the experience it offers.

Literature doesn't simply comment on human experience. It is itself an experience—an act by one mind that is reenacted in the minds of all who read it well. Poetry is the form of literature that depends most on the rhythms and sounds of normal speech, and on the devices of compression and comparison that enable it, once inside the mind, to explode there with a power of meaning that can literally make one's day or even change one's life. In other words, a poem not only *says* much in little space; it also *is* much.

The first two sections of the book focus on the essentials of any literary act: a situation or subject, a speaker, an audience, and a particular attitude toward all three expressing itself as tone. These combine to give the dramatic experience that is the poem. The third section deals with the poet's dependence on the normal rhythms and sound patterns of language: how they are regularized and manipulated is illustrated in some detail. The fourth section spells out the poet's shorthand—the devices of compression that are implicit in all uses of language, but most strikingly in poetry: overstatement, understatement, irony, paradox, metaphor, and the other sorts of comparison and contrast.

The final section is a collection of poems for further reading. Portions of some of these poems are used for study and illustration of particular points made earlier in the book; others are entirely fresh. The poems are arranged chronologically from the sixteenth century to the present, and provide a ground for extending the insights developed earlier in the book.

CONTENTS

SOUND   *111*

IV Devices of Compression: *The Poet's Shorthand* ············ 123

OVERSTATEMENT   *123*

UNDERSTATEMENT   *134*

IRONY AND PARADOX   *138*

INTRODUCTION
TO THE
POEM

INTRODUCTION

Poets are the athletes of language. What we call poetic skill is the ability to get the most out of certain capacities of language that we all use in less interesting ways—just as athletic skill in boxing, baseball, dancing, swimming, or tennis is the ability to get the most out of certain bodily capacities we all use every day but not so powerfully or so gracefully.

The secret of both kinds of skill, the poet's and the athlete's, is coordination. Many elements must be made to cooperate to a single end. In the poet's case, the elements that must enter into cooperation are (1) the subject, (2) the situation, (3) the patterns of rhythm and sound, and (4) the various verbal patterns and techniques that evoke a maximum of significance from a minimum of words. We will look at each of these in turn.

Poetry is first and foremost a performer's art. Its life is in the spoken language, in the application of normal speech sounds and rhythms to gain varied and subtle ends. To enjoy it you must speak and hear it—either out loud or in your head—and this is, fortunately, a skill that can be learned. We feel that the best way to develop that skill is to treat poems as performances—to read them aloud over and over, trying different emphases, playing with different phrasing, letting the rhythms echo in the head, and so getting to know a number of poems so well they'll never be forgotten.

Like singing in the shower, performing a poem requires only a self-audience—and the pleasure is infinitely repeatable. Unlike singing in the shower, added pleasure comes from reading or reciting in front of an audience, either a handful at home or several handsful in the classroom. Whichever way, the important thing is to get some poems into your verbal memory—singing around in your head like favorite tunes—and the more the better.

1

If you play a musical instrument or sing in some sort of choral group, you know the repeated pleasure that comes from having a piece so much at your command that you find yourself refining your performance of it every time you go through it. Actors don't grow tired of a good part, even if they play it night after night and twice on Wednesdays and Saturdays. The basketball player who has perfected a jump shot could throw it up all day without getting bored. The same thing, over and over again.

But is it the same thing? Each performer would hedge on the question: "In a sense it's the same thing, but only in the most superficial way. It may seem monotonously similar to anyone watching, but to me it's different every time I do it. I've got it under control—could do it in my sleep—but that's when I like it most: when I don't have to think about what I'm doing, when I can just enjoy doing it well and even fool around with it because I know I have it under control."

There are thousands of skills that various people are expert enough in to enjoy in the way we're talking about, and *reading* poetry—aloud or silently —is one of them. The demands it makes on a reader to do more with it than find out its literal sense require practice, repeated performance, familiarity, ease—all the qualities that make skills ultimately enjoyable. Nobody plays the piano well or makes jump shots consistently without a lot of practice and without the early frustration of being a bungler. The problem is to get past the stage of feeling strange and inept—the temptation to say that the pleasure in doing something well is not worth the time and effort it demands. If you do with this book what we suggest you do, you won't be a bungler for long.

Two considerations have guided our selection of poems:

(1) We have picked poems that read easily. That doesn't mean that they're immediately understood or that they're simple-minded, but that they have an instantly recognizable rhythmic flow, a "music" that grabs in an intriguing way, a pleasing regularity of language form that almost invites us not to worry about whether we fully understand *all* they say. It's foolish to argue that it doesn't make any difference what a poem "says"—after all, language is meant to convey meaning as well as make a noise—but it's just as foolish to worry a poem to a frazzle to get all its "meaning" out. There is decided delight in the sound of words that sing together, and many a poem complex in meaning can delight even very young children with its verbal music—though they may make little "sense" of it.

(2) We have also picked many of the finest poems in the language, written over a spread of several centuries. This is not a plea for "appreciation of the classics"; our feeling is simply that those we have chosen will hit you where you live. If in the process of becoming familiar with them you also become familiar with some of the great poets of the English-speaking world, so much the better for you.

The poems in Sections I-IV are accompanied by a series of "Considerations" that we hope will deepen your initial responses. Though framed as questions, we intend them only as aids to reading and discussion. They are not testing devices, nor are they puzzles with a discoverable solution.

I
THE POEM
AS SUBJECT

THE SUBJECT OF A POEM MAY BE ANYTHING WHATEVER

The subject matter of poetry is as broad as life itself. It isn't chiefly concerned, as some anthologies of the recent past would lead us to suppose, with moonlight and roses, mother, home, and sweetheart, or the horns of Elfland faintly blowing. On the contrary, it includes every kind of mood, problem, and experience that human beings know: terror, hatred, madness, and despair; love, hope, compassion, joy; birth and death; sex and marriage; youth and age; city, country, animal, machine; the ugly, the beautiful, the brutal, the tender, the solemn, the humorous.

The aspect of humor in poetry needs particular emphasis, for too often people today are unaware that good poetry can laugh—or smile, or chuckle; and much more poetry of this kind should be published in the books we read in school. Not because somebody wants to show us that poetry can be bearable, but because laughter is specifically human and should play its part in education. What we laugh at is a sign of what we are, of the extent to which we're civilized.

Here are a few specimens of laughing poetry, from the chuckle to the smile, which any civilized person should be able to enjoy. If you enjoy all of them, you'll enjoy this book. If you don't, you need it.

[1]   *Lines for a Christmas Card*
           HILAIRE BELLOC (1870–1953)

           May all my enemies go to hell,
           Noel, Noel, Noel, Noel.

5

[2]   ## *This Is the Grave of Mike O'Day*
ANONYMOUS

This is the grave of Mike O'Day,
Who died maintaining his right of way.
His right was clear, his will was strong,
But he's just as dead as if he'd been wrong.

[3]   ## *Epitaph*
WRITTEN BY A TWELFTH-GRADE PUPIL

Here lies her
Gone and departing
She failed English grammar
And died broken hearting.

[4]   ## *Epigram*
Engraved on the Collar of a Dog I Gave to
His Royal Highness

ALEXANDER POPE (1688–1744)

I am His Highness' Dog at Kew;
Pray tell me, Sir, whose Dog are you?

[5]   ## *The Gray Squirrel*
HUMBERT WOLFE (1885–1940)

Like a small gray
coffeepot
sits the squirrel.
He is not

all he should be,   5
kills by dozens
trees, and eats
his red-brown cousins.

The keeper, on the
other hand   10

, who shot him, is
a Christian, and

loves his enemies,
which shows
the squirrel was not   15
one of those.

[6]   *On an Ecdysiast*

JOHN CIARDI (1916–   )

She stripped herself of all except pretense.
By nature she and Nature lived to feud
over two words. Her life explains their sense:
born naked into the world, she left it nude.

[7]   ***You Are You***

SANDRA BOYNTON (1953–   )

You are you,
and I am I.
We are alone, together.
And if the I that is I
is not in harmony with
the you that is you,
then the we that is us
will become the them that was,
or were.

CONSIDERATIONS

1   Why is the title of poem 1 essential? What kinds of lines usually go on Christmas cards? What attitude are Christians supposed to take toward their enemies? How can you prove that the poet is not a grouch but a man with a good sense of humor?

2   What is the pun that makes poem 2 humorous?

3   What connection is there between the subject of poem 3 and the way it is written?

4   In poem 4, to whom is the question in the second line addressed? What clue tells us it's not addressed to another dog? Then why is the word "dog" used in line 2? What does it mean as used there? What comment does it make on courtiers? Use the word "dog" in a sentence of your own that will show the meaning it has in line 2.

5   In poem 5:
    a. What are shown to be the shortcomings of the gray squirrel?
    b. What are shown to be the shortcomings of the keeper? What is he the keeper of? Why does he shoot the squirrel?
    c. Which is regarded in the poem as the less admirable—squirrel or keeper? How do you know?
    d. How does a squirrel resemble a coffeepot? What does the comparison tell us about the speaker's attitude toward the squirrel? How would our understanding of the attitude be changed if the comparison read: "Like a cocky hoodlum . . ."?
    e. In what sense is the poem humorous? In what sense is it not?

6   In poem 6:
    a. Look up *ecdysiast* in a dictionary. As a whole, does line 1 tell us anything about the "she" of the poem that the word ecdysiast does not? If so, what?
    b. "Nature" and "she," the poem tells us, "feud"—disagree—about "two words." What are those words? What do they have to do with the ecdysiast's profession? Which of the two does "she" favor? Which does "Nature" favor? Which do *you* favor? Why? (Does a dictionary help in defining the difference for you? Why or why not?)
    c. Write a paragraph showing that line 4 is simply a different way of making the point that is made by line 1. (What does "all except pretense" mean?)
    d. "Born naked into the world" is doubtless meant to remind us of the ways of looking at life which we inherit from sources like the following: (1) "And they were both naked, the man and his wife,

and were not ashamed" (Genesis 2:25); "And he said, Naked came I out of my mother's womb, and naked shall I return thither" (Job 1:21). How do these ways of looking at life differ from those implied in "nude"? On what grounds can they be associated with *Nature*?

e. The form of the poem is that of a verse epitaph—a concise commemorative inscription for a tomb. What specific elements in the poem remind you of other such inscriptions that you may have seen? In what ways is the association of epitaphs and tombs with a stripteaser funny? Why is the title "On an Ecdysiast" funnier than "On a Stripteaser"?

7 Why is poem 7 funny? You've seen hundreds (thousands) of "poems" like it on greeting cards, and they take themselves very seriously. People (not poets) churn them out every day. How is this one the same as those thousands, yet different? Is this writer a poet? Why or why not?

THE SUBJECT OF A POEM IS NOT THE SAME THING AS ITS THEME

i

A poem's *subject matter* is whatever the poem talks about. In poem 5, above, the subject includes the habits of the gray squirrel, the act of the keeper in shooting it, and so on. The *theme* of a poem, on the other hand, is its "idea," its *generalized* content, which it is possible to state with various degrees of generality. Thus one could say that the theme of poem 5 is that animals follow the law of the jungle and destroy—but that people are worse because they destroy while pretending to follow a higher law. Or one could say, much more generally, that the theme is the hypocrisy of human beings.

In poem 6, the *subject matter* has to do with a now-dead stripper who is represented as having had a life-long argument with Nature about nakedness versus nudity. The *theme*, on the other hand, is a point about honesty, and the contamination of honesty by any form of pretense, which the poem *uses* the stripper to convey.

In the following poem, much of the subject matter is declared in the title. Two neighboring New England farmers are out walking along their stone boundary-wall in the spring, each on his own side, and as they go they replace the stones that the "frozen-ground-swell" of winter has dislodged. One of them ventures to suggest that the wall is hardly necessary. The other replies that good fences make good neighbors. The first speaker then asks: Why so—unless you need to wall something out? The second speaker doesn't answer; he simply repeats what he had said before, "Good fences make good neighbors." This, in brief, is the subject matter of the poem. What is its theme?

Mending Wall

                ROBERT FROST (1874–1963)

Something there is that doesn't love a wall,
That sends the frozen-ground-swell under it,
And spills the upper boulders in the sun;
And makes gaps even two can pass abreast.
The work of hunters is another thing: 5
I have come after them and made repair
Where they have left not one stone on a stone,
But they would have the rabbit out of hiding,
To please the yelping dogs. The gaps I mean,
No one has seen them made or heard them made,   10
But at spring mending-time we find them there.
I let my neighbor know beyond the hill;
And on a day we meet to walk the line
And set the wall between us once again.
We keep the wall between us as we go.   15
To each the boulders that have fallen to each.
And some are loaves and some so nearly balls
We have to use a spell to make them balance:
"Stay where you are until our backs are turned!"
We wear our fingers rough with handling them.   20
Oh, just another kind of outdoor game,
One on a side. It comes to little more:
There where it is we do not need the wall:
He is all pine and I am apple orchard.
My apple trees will never get across   25
And eat the cones under his pines, I tell him.
He only says, "Good fences make good neighbors."
Spring is the mischief in me, and I wonder
If I could put a notion in his head:
"*Why* do they make good neighbors? Isn't it   30
Where there are cows? But here there are no cows.
Before I built a wall I'd ask to know
What I was walling in or walling out,
And to whom I was like to give offense.
Something there is that doesn't love a wall,   35

That wants it down." I could say "Elves" to him,
But it's not elves exactly, and I'd rather
He said it for himself. I see him there
Bringing a stone grasped firmly by the top
In each hand, like an old-stone savage armed.   40
He moves in darkness as it seems to me,
Not of woods only and the shade of trees.
He will not go behind his father's saying,
And he likes having thought of it so well
He says again, "Good fences make good neighbors."   45

CONSIDERATIONS

1 How many things or persons are mentioned in the poem that apparently do not love a wall? What would you say the "something" is that is referred to in lines 1 and 35? What is implied about the nature of this "something" by lines 36–37?

2 A current comic saying, with which you're probably familiar, runs, "Don't confuse me with facts; my mind's made up." Does this saying seem to you to be in any way illustrated in the poem? Where? Be specific.

3 What do lines 38–42 tell us about the theme? What is the "darkness" referred to in line 41? Is it a darkness that we're all likely to be surrounded by, sometime? Give an example.

ii

After each of the following three poems there is a series of questions. The last question in each series will ask you to state the *subject matter* of the poem, and then to put into your own words what the *theme* is.

[2]   *Cliff Klingenhagen*
               EDWIN ARLINGTON ROBINSON (1869–1935)

Cliff Klingenhagen had me in to dine
With him one day; and after soup and meat,
And all the other things there were to eat,
Cliff took two glasses and filled one with wine

And one with wormwood. Then, without a sign   5
For me to choose at all, he took the draught
Of bitterness himself, and lightly quaffed
It off, and said the other one was mine.
And when I asked him what the deuce he meant
By doing that, he only looked at me   10
And smiled, and said it was a way of his.
And though I know the fellow, I have spent
Long time a-wondering when I shall be
As happy as Cliff Klingenhagen is.

CONSIDERATIONS

1   What is wormwood? In what ways are wine and wormwood different? What would you say each represents in the poem?

2   How does Cliff Klingenhagen's behavior warrant the use of the word "happy" in the last line of the poem? What does he do that should make him happy?

3   What is the subject matter of the poem? What is its theme? Why does Cliff Klingenhagen's attitude bring happiness?

[3]   *Bredon Hill*

A. E. HOUSMAN (1859–1936)

In summertime on Bredon°
    The bells they sound so clear;
Round both the shires they ring them
    In steeples far and near,
    A happy noise to hear.   5

Here of a Sunday morning
    My love and I would lie,
And see the colored counties,
    And hear the larks so high
    About us in the sky.   10

°**Bredon:** a British hill overlooking two shires (counties).

The bells would ring to call her
   In valleys miles away:
"Come all to church, good people;
   Good people, come and pray."
But here my love would stay.   15

And I would turn and answer
   Among the springing thyme,
"Oh, peal upon our wedding,
   And we will hear the chime,
And come to church in time."   20

But when the snows at Christmas
   On Bredon top were strown,
My love rose up so early
   And stole out unbeknown
And went to church alone.   25

They tolled the one bell only,
   Groom there was none to see,
The mourners followed after,
   And so to church went she,
And would not wait for me.   30

The bells they sound on Bredon,
   And still the steeples hum.
"Come all to church, good people,"—
   Oh, noisy bells, be dumb;
I hear you, I will come.   35

CONSIDERATIONS

1 What two times of the year are dealt with in the poem? Why is the
   sound of the bells a "happy noise" in the first stanza? When do the
   lovers intend to go to church together? Why does the speaker's loved
   one in fact go alone? What word in line 11 hints that she may be the
   first to go?

2   What did the speaker think the bells were reminding him of when he
    lay on Bredon Hill? What does he discover they are also reminding
    him of by the end of the poem? When he says he will obey the bells
    (line 35), what does he mean?

3   What is the subject matter of the poem? What is its theme?

[4]   *The Big I*

JOHN HALL WHEELOCK (1886–1978)

A bird with a big eye
In at my window poked his head,
And fixed me with a big eye.
"Who are you? What do you want?" I said.
"Me? You mean you don't know me?" he made reply,   5
"Why, I am I. Who are you?"
"I, too, am I," I bashfully admitted.
Now here was a big I-dea to work upon,
For if each one is I, must we not all be one?
Then I am one in all, and all are one in me.   10
I observed, thinking it over carefully,
That I wondered, this being true,
What made us feel so separate, so alone.
"*I* did," shouted the bird,
And I turned to strangle him, but he was flown.   15

CONSIDERATIONS

1   State in your own words the "big I-dea" that is referred to in line 8
    and elaborated in lines 9–10. Just how does the experience described
    in lines 1–7 raise this "I-dea"? What evidence from our normal expe-
    rience as human beings is brought forward in line 13 to contradict
    the conclusion in line 10?

2   In lines 6–7, as the two speakers confront each other, both say, "'I am I."
    Is the conclusion in line 10 the only conclusion that can emerge from
    this situation? How does the situation prepare the reader for what
    is said in line 13? in line 15? What does the emphasis on "I" throughout

the poem have to do with line 15? How would you relate this emphasis to the bird's "big eye"?

3 Discuss the merit of each of the following sentences as an interpretation of the poem: (a) The poem is about the paradoxical character of the human ego, which is both selfish and unselfish, and which longs both for individualism and community; (b) The poem is about the difference between philosophy and experience, reason and feeling; (c) The poem is about the human world's irreconcilability with the world of nature represented in the bird.

4 What is the subject matter of the poem? What is its theme?

THE MEANING OF A POEM IS NOT THE SAME THING AS ITS SUBJECT OR ITS THEME

i

The theme of a poem is part of its meaning, just as is its subject matter. But neither subject matter nor theme nor both together make the whole meaning. The whole meaning of a poem is the whole poem as it stands, and nothing less.

This fact must be stressed because one of the commonest misconceptions of inexperienced readers is that a poem contains a meaning in the same way that a pill bottle contains a pill: you swallow the pill and throw the bottle away. Nothing could be farther from the truth. Good poems are much more like people—or plants—than they are like pill bottles. To be sure, it's often *convenient,* as we have just seen, to talk of the *theme* of a poem and of its *subject* as if these were separable things that the rest of the poem exists only to convey. In the same way, it's *convenient* to talk of a man's or a woman's "character," "temperament," "intelligence." But just as none of these abstract words can substitute for the whole person, who is always flesh, blood, and bone—a person with eyes and hair of a certain color, a brown mole behind the right ear, and a passion for fried parsnips —so no theme or subject can substitute for the whole poem. The whole meaning of a poem such as "The Gray Squirrel," which you have already read, is not simply that squirrels are destructive and that keepers shoot them, nor that human beings are hypocrites who preach one thing and practice another, nor even a combination of these. It's this theme as modified by a great many features of poems that we have so far not mentioned: the poem's speaker, audience, tone, rhythm, meter, and many more. To illustrate specifically, meaning is substantially modified in "The Gray Squirrel" by (among other things) the comparison of squirrel and coffee-pot with which the poem opens. This comparison is not only arresting but consciously comic. It begets in us from the very start an amused attitude toward squirrels (rather than, say, a hostile attitude), and it thus persuades us to see the squirrel as something of a charming "oddball," damaging in some respects, no doubt, but harmless to human beings, and surely not a creature to be lightheartedly destroyed.

Consider in this connection two poems that have something in common as to theme, but differ enormously as to subject and even more as to their whole meaning.

[1]   *God's Will for You and Me*

ANONYMOUS

Just to be tender, just to be true,
Just to be glad the whole day through,
Just to be merciful, just to be mild,
Just to be trustful as a child,
Just to be gentle and kind and sweet,   5
Just to be helpful with willing feet,
Just to be cheery when things go wrong,
Just to drive sadness away with a song,
Whether the hour is dark or bright,
Just to be loyal to God and right,   10
Just to believe that God knows best,
Just in his promises ever to rest—
Just to let love be our daily key,
That is God's Will for you and me.

[2]   *A Man Who Had Fallen Among Thieves*°

E. E. CUMMINGS (1894–1962)

a man who had fallen among thieves
lay by the roadside on his back
dressed in fifteenthrate ideas
wearing a round jeer for a hat

°**Title:** See Luke 10:30–37.

fate per a somewhat more than less   5
emancipated evening
had in return for consciousness
endowed him with a changeless grin

whereon a dozen staunch and leal°
citizens did graze at pause   10
then fired by hypercivic zeal
sought newer pastures or because

swaddled with a frozen brook
of pinkest vomit out of eyes
which noticed nobody he looked   15
as if he did not care to rise

one hand did nothing on the vest
its wideflung friend clenched weakly dirt
while the mute trouserfly confessed
a button solemnly inert.   20

Brushing from whom the stiffened puke
i put him all into my arms
and staggered banged with terror through
a million billion trillion stars.

Poem 1 is an uplift poem of the sort that used to be printed on edify-
ing calendars and nailed to the bathroom wall beside the shaving mirror.
The weakness of such poetry is that it falsifies life by making matters that
are very complicated and very difficult appear simple and easy. "Just to
be merciful" is a case in point. The sentiment is noble. But how does one
go about being "merciful" without destroying justice? Or just without
destroying mercy? The question is one of the profoundest puzzles that
every human community—and every classroom—have to face. The poet
shows no awareness of the puzzle. Or consider: "Just to be loyal to God
and right." This is also a noble idea—but in practice it's not always possible to know whether we *are* right, and it's dangerous to be too sure

---

°**leal:** loyal.

about it. The men who hanged the "witches" at Salem believed intensely that they were right. So did the slaveholders in both North and South. Most Americans think now that it brought more good than evil to drop the atomic bomb on Hiroshima in 1945. Most Japanese do not agree. Who is right? So here again the poet shows no true understanding of what his own words mean. And because he doesn't, his *intended* meaning is eventually undermined altogether by his actual *words*. His intended meaning in the poem as a whole might be expressed, "How little God asks of us! Just to be tender . . . ," and so on. But by the time we come to the end of the poem, his words, when we think about them, have departed so far from this intention that they actually appear to be saying, almost with a cynical sneer, "All God asks of us is the impossible. Just to be tender . . ."

Poem 2 is a lot harder to understand at first sight than poem 1, but precisely because it has something to say. It's based, as its title tells us, on the parable of the Good Samaritan, a man of a despised people who gives aid to a traveler "who had fallen among thieves," been stripped of his clothes, and left half dead by the roadside. The story tells us that a priest and a Levite—men of greater respectability and standing in the community—see the wounded man, but they pass by on the other side. But when the Samaritan comes along, he tends the man's wounds, lodges him at an inn, and leaves money with the landlord of the inn for further care after the Samaritan himself has gone. The poem's aim is to make us see and feel this situation afresh—in modern terms, the terms in which we ourselves will meet with it.

The author of poem 2 does not, like the author of poem 1, falsify reality by making what is hard or questionable seem easy and clear. The victim in poem 2, so far as we can tell, is not an outstanding or even an admirable man: he appears to have "fifteenthrate" ideas and an attitude toward society that can be described as "a round jeer." There is certainly no social credit to be gained by rescuing him. Far from it. He has been on a drunken binge (5–6), wears the exasperating silly grin of the dead drunk (8), is half unbuttoned (19–20), shows no interest in being helped (15–16), and probably, thanks to the "pinkest vomit" (14), smells disgusting. Several "staunch and leal" citizens have already looked at him and passed by (9–16). But the speaker of the poem, with a lunge of pity that overcomes his physical revulsion (emphasized in the strong words "stiffened puke") accepts the full nature of humankind with *all* its capacities, both for degradation and for greatness—" i put him all into my arms"—and by doing so finds he has entered a new dimension, even a new world:

> and staggered banged with terror through
> a million billion trillion stars.

CONSIDERATIONS

1 Do you see any other phrases in poem 1 besides the two already singled out that indicate that the poet is falsifying by making what is hard, complex, or impossible sound simple, or what is undesirable sound good? Is cheeriness (line 7), for example, necessarily a desirable reaction when things go wrong?

2 Does poem 1 have any characteristics, in addition to the thoughtlessness of its words, that might be described as childish and silly? What are they?

3 In poem 2, the term "emancipated" is used to describe a drunken binge. Does it seem to you the sort of term that is suited to such use? Could it be an example of one of those "fifteenthrate ideas" by which the victim apparently has directed his life? What was he "emancipated" from?

4 The citizens in poem 2 are said to be "staunch and leal." What are we to suppose they are loyal *to?* They are "fired by hypercivic zeal." Zeal for what?

5 It has been said that poem 2 is about the eternal conflict between the conscience of the individual and the conventions of society. Can you see why? Which side is the poet on? Which side is the New Testament parable on?

6 "Emancipated," as we have seen above, is the kind of word a drunken man might use to conceal from himself the real nature of his alcoholism. "Staunch" and "leal" are old-fashioned words such as the citizens might use to conceal from themselves their real motives for passing by on the other side. What does the poem suggest the real motives are? What are these citizens likened to by the words "graze" in line 10 and "pastures" in line 12?

7 In line 22, the poet makes the speaker speak of himself with a small instead of a capital *I*. Does this small *i* have any significance? In line 23 why do you suppose the speaker describes himself as "banged with terror"?

ii

Here are four more poems in which subject and theme are clearly modified by each poet's handling.

[3]   *Delight in Disorder*
                    ROBERT HERRICK (1591–1674)

> A sweet disorder in the dress
> Kindles in clothes a wantonness:
> A lawn° about the shoulders thrown
> Into a fine distraction:
> An erring lace, which here and there   5
> Enthralls the crimson stomacher:°
> A cuff neglectful, and thereby
> Ribands to flow confusedly:
> A winning wave (deserving note)
> In the tempestuous petticoat: 10
> A careless shoestring, in whose tie
> I see a wild civility:
> Do more bewitch me, than when art
> Is too precise in every part.

CONSIDERATIONS

1   What details in lines 3–12 make specific the "sweet disorder" spoken
    of in line 1?

2   Why does the disorder "more bewitch" the speaker than would "art"
    that is "too precise"?

3   What is the subject matter of the poem? What is its theme?

4   Try to indicate as specifically as possible how the choice of words
    qualifies the theme. Consider, for instance, "sweet disorder," "wanton-
    ness," "fine distraction," "erring lace," "winning wave," "tempestuous
    petticoat," and "wild civility." What is the nature of the "delight" that
    the speaker finds in disorder? Is the disorder itself "artful"?

°**lawn:** sheer linen.   °**stomacher:** the center front section, usually em-
broidered, of the waist of a woman's dress.

[4]   *Bells for John Whiteside's Daughter*

JOHN CROWE RANSOM (1888–1974)

There was such speed in her little body,
And such lightness in her footfall,
It is no wonder her brown study
Astonishes us all.

Her wars were bruited in our high window.   5
We looked among orchard trees and beyond,
Where she took arms against her shadow,
Or harried unto the pond

The lazy geese, like a snow cloud
Dripping their snow on the green grass,   10
Tricking and stopping, sleepy and proud,
Who cried in goose, Alas,

For the tireless heart within the little
Lady with rod that made them rise
From their noon apple-dreams, and scuttle   15
Goose-fashion under the skies!

But now go the bells, and we are ready;
In one house we are sternly stopped
To say we are vexed at her brown study,
Lying so primly propped.   20

CONSIDERATIONS

1   What does a "brown study" usually mean? What does it mean in this case? Why does the girl's stillness seem astonishing?

2   What activities of the young girl does the speaker recall? Why does he refer to them as "wars"? In what sense were they "wars"? In what sense not?

3   How does the length of the sentence that occupies stanzas two, three, and four help convey the "tireless" character of the "little lady with rod"? What is the attitude of the geese toward their disturber?

4 "Astonishes" (line 4) and "vexed" (line 19) indicate a response different from the one we might ordinarily expect to the death of a young
   girl. So does the humorous treatment of the harried geese. So do
   phrases like "sternly stopped" and "primly propped." What is the
   speaker plainly seeking to avoid in treating the little girl's death?

5 Show how the way the subject matter is handled defines the meaning
   of the poem.

[5]   *A Narrow Fellow in the Grass*
                 EMILY DICKINSON (1830–1886)

          A narrow fellow in the grass
          Occasionally rides;
          You may have met him,—did you not?
          His notice sudden is.

          The grass divides as with a comb,   5
          A spotted shaft is seen;
          And then it closes at your feet
          And opens further on.

          He likes a boggy acre,
          A floor too cool for corn.   10
          But when a boy, and barefoot,
          I more than once at noon

          Have passed, I thought, a whiplash
          Unbraiding in the sun,—
          When, stooping to secure it,   15
          It wrinkled, and was gone.

          Several of nature's people
          I know, and they know me;
          I feel for them a transport
          Of cordiality;   20

But never met this fellow,
Attended or alone,
Without a tighter breathing,
And zero at the bone.

CONSIDERATIONS

1   What is the subject matter of the poem? Who or what is the "narrow fellow in the grass"? What details of the way he acts identify him?

2   Is there anything in the first five stanzas to suggest that the "narrow fellow" would cause the "tighter breathing,/And zero at the bone" mentioned in the last two lines? Consider what is suggested by the use of such terms as "narrow fellow," "comb," "shaft," "whiplash," and "wrinkled"—and such odd syntax as "His notice sudden is." How do these seemingly whimsical descriptive phrases contrast with, and at the same time support, the last two lines to give a special meaning to the encounter?

3   What famous encounter in the Bible helps to account for this special meaning? Why?

[6]   *The Sea Turtle and the Shark*

MELVIN B. TOLSON (1900–1966)

Strange but true is the story
of the sea-turtle and the shark—
the instinctive drive of the weak to survive
in the oceanic dark.
            Driven,   5
               riven
            by hunger
      from abyss to shoal,
sometimes the shark swallows
      the sea-turtle whole.   10
   "The sly reptilian marine
         withdraws,
      into the shell

of his undersea craft,
his leathery head and the rapacious claws   15
that can rip
a rhinoceros' hide
or strip
a crocodile to fare-thee-well;
now,   20
inside the shark,
the sea-turtle begins the churning seesaws
of his descent into pelagic hell;
then . . . *then,*
with ravenous jaws   25
that can cut sheet steel scrap,
the sea-turtle gnaws
. . . and gnaws . . . and gnaws . . .
his way in a way that appalls—
his way to freedom,   30
beyond the vomiting dark,
beyond the stomach walls
of the shark."

CONSIDERATIONS

1 The subject matter of this poem is obvious: the shark swallows the sea-turtle, and the sea-turtle gnaws his way to freedom, destroying the shark. What causes does the poem assign to the shark's action? To the sea-turtle's? By what means does the poem communicate the compelling power of these forces? What does the sea-setting contribute to our sense of their power?

2 What indications can you discover in the poem that the subject matter may not be all that the poet is interested in conveying to us—that the shark's and sea-turtle's blind destruction of each other may incorporate a theme more immediately relevant to *human* concerns? Which of the following ways of stating something more is best supported by the poem's actual details: (1) Our world is a place where only blind instinctive drives to survive ultimately count; (2) Our world everywhere presents us with the paradox of the destroyer who is destroyed by his own rapacity, or by his own arrogant use of power;

(3) The black ghetto, swallowed up in a rapacious white society, will inevitably destroy that society in achieving its freedom. Choose one of these interpretations and defend it in a paragraph or two.

3 In Shakespeare's *King Lear*, a character sees humanity (as in Tolson's poem) preying on itself "like monsters of the deep"; and Thomas Hobbes, a seventeenth-century philosopher, conceived human society as a "war *of* all *on* all." What are your own views on this matter? Is society simply a polite mask beneath which men prey on each other? or a brotherhood? or something in between? Do *you* behave like the shark and sea-turtle? If yes, what drives you? Hunger? Greed? Cruelty? Stupidity? If no, what prevents you? Fear? Social habit? Natural affection? Religious training? Ability to imagine how another feels? When did you last try to imagine how others feel? What success did you have?

4 Now that you have considered both subject-matter and theme in Tolson's poem, consider the *particular* shape that it gives these by its formal characteristics. What elements of grim humor may be detected in the word choices generally? in the comparisons in lines 11 and 14? in the parallel established between the situation described in lines 6–7 and that described in lines 27–33? in the exaggeration of lines 25–26? Do rhythm and rhyme achieve any effects that seem appropriate to the story being told? Can you account for the mixture of very short with longer lines? for the rise in intensity of feeling and attitude that seems to take place between line 1 and lines 28–33? Trace the rise in detail.

iii

Compare the following three poems, whose themes are much alike. Then answer the questions at the end of each. As you read them, note carefully the ways in which the "meaning" of each is affected by the poet's individual way of handling the common theme.

[7]   *Without Benefit of Declaration*

LANGSTON HUGHES (1902–1967)

Listen here, Joe,
Don't you know

That tomorrow
You got to go
Out yonder where   5
The steel winds blow?

Listen here, kid,
It's been said
Tomorrow you'll be dead
Out there where   10
The snow is lead.
Don't ask me why
Just go ahead and die.

Hidden from the sky
Out yonder you'll lie: 15
A medal to your family—
In exchange for
A guy.

Mama, don't cry.

CONSIDERATIONS

1   In each of the poem's three stanzas, nature's world is contrasted with
    man's world as seen in time of war. How and where is this contrast
    achieved in each case? What is the purpose of it?

2   The last line is set apart from the body of the poem. Why so? What
    new perspective on man's world does it bring before us? What sort
    of comment does this new perspective make on the activities of lines
    1–18?

3   Most of the poem is addressed to a "Joe," who is also a "kid," who
    does not anywhere make a reply. Does this add to or detract from
    the poem's effect? Explain.

[8] *Dulce et Decorum Est*°
WILFRED OWEN (1893–1918)

Bent double, like old beggars under sacks,
Knock-kneed, coughing like hags, we cursed through sludge,
Till on the haunting flares we turned our backs,
And toward our distant rest began to trudge.
Men marched asleep. Many had lost their boots, 5
But limped on, blood-shod. All went lame, all blind;
Drunk with fatigue; deaf even to the hoots
Of gas-shells dropping softly behind.

Gas! Gas! Quick, boys!—An ecstasy of fumbling,
Fitting the clumsy helmets just in time, 10
But someone still was yelling out and stumbling
And floundering like a man in fire or lime.—
Dim through the misty panes and thick green light,
As under a green sea, I saw him drowning.

In all my dreams before my helpless sight 15
He plunges at me, guttering, choking, drowning.

If in some smothering dreams, you too could pace
Behind the wagon that we flung him in,
And watch the white eyes writhing in his face,
His hanging face, like a devil's sick of sin; 20
If you could hear, at every jolt, the blood
Come gargling from the froth-corrupted lungs,
Bitter as the cud
Of vile, incurable sores on innocent tongues,—
My friend, you would not tell with such high zest 25
To children ardent for some desperate glory,
The old Lie: *Dulce et decorum est
Pro patria mori.*

°*Dulce et decorum est [pro patria mori]*: Sweet and fitting it is to die for
one's country; a quotation from the Roman poet Horace.

CONSIDERATIONS

1   How has the speaker created a sense of utter weariness and despair in the first stanza? What kind of men have these soldiers become?

2   What are the men headed toward when the gas attack occurs? What specifically happens to the one man who cannot get his gas mask on in time? How do lines 13–14 prepare for the "smothering dreams" described in the last stanza?

3   The speaker is not describing something that is happening, but something that has happened. Why does the memory of it haunt him? Why is he telling it? To whom?

4   The subject matter is the memory of the horrible death of one man in war. What is the theme?

5   The speaker argues that the sentiment from Horace is a "Lie." Was there anything to be said on the other side in Horace's day? Is there now? Why or why not?

[9]   *plato told him*

            E. E. CUMMINGS (1894–1962)

plato told

him:he couldn't
believe it(jesus

told him;he
wouldn't believe   5
it)lao

tsze
certainly. told
him,and general
(yes   10
mam)
sherman;

and even
(believe it
or   15

not)you
told him:i told
him;we told him
(he didn't believe it,no

sir)it took   20
a nipponized bit of
the old sixth

avenue
el;in the top of his head:to tell

him   25

CONSIDERATIONS

What Plato, Jesus, Lao-tsze, General Sherman, and "even . . . you . . .
[and] I . . . [and] we told him" was, in General Sherman's words: "War
is hell." (General Sherman made several devastating marches through
parts of the South near the close of the Civil War and was felt by South-
erners to have put his view of war into practice.) The reference in lines
20–25 is to the fact that the Sixth Avenue El (elevated train tracks running
along Sixth Avenue in New York City) was torn down and sold in part to
the Japanese (Nipponese) in the 1930's as scrap metal, which they used to
manufacture armaments.

1   Who is the "him" of lines 2, 4, 9, 17, 18, and 25?

2   What are the nationalities and approximate dates of Plato? Jesus?
    Lao-tsze? What idea would be lost if the three names were all of one
    nationality (for example, Moses, Isaiah, Jesus) or of one period?

3   Why isn't "he" convinced? What does convince him? In what condi-
    tion is he when he at last learns? What does this slowness suggest
    about "his" long-run future?

4 The arrangement of words in the poem seeks to act out the thrust of telling and the counterthrust of not believing. How? What words or phrases are repeated? In what pattern? What marked change in the pattern takes place in lines 20–25 to act out the change that has taken place in "him"? The poem ends with a powerful emphasis on "him," which stands alone in line 25. Can you see why?

5 What is gained by the change from "couldn't" in line 2 to "wouldn't" in line 5? What repetition in lines 16–18 brings to a climax the effort to persuade "him" by reason? What rhyme in line 24 emphasizes the change in pattern mentioned in question 4?

6 How does the intrusion of "yes mam" between "general" and "sherman" suggest surprise that a general would say such a thing? What other intrusions serve the same end? What is the purpose of such intrusions?

7 What is the theme of the poem? How is the theme the same as that of "Dulce et Decorum Est"? In what sense is it different? What are some of the factors that make the total meaning different? Consider in the two poems (a) the length and kind of sentence and (b) the choice of words. (Which poem is breezier? Why?)

8 Write a short paper arguing that "Dulce et Decorum Est" is effective by what it puts in and "plato told him" by what it leaves out.

iv

In the following two poems, consider what the relationship is between the subject matter and the meaning of each.

[10]   *The Sloth*
THEODORE ROETHKE (1908–1963)

In moving-slow he has no Peer.
You ask him something in his Ear,
He thinks about it for a Year;

And, then, before he says a Word
There, upside down (unlike a Bird),   5
He will assume that you have Heard—

A most Ex-as-per-at-ing Lug.
But should you call his manner Smug,
He'll sigh and give his Branch a Hug;

Then off again to Sleep he goes,   10
Still swaying gently by his Toes,
And you just *know* he knows he knows.

CONSIDERATIONS

1   What makes the sloth "Ex-as-per-at-ing"? Is being "Ex-as-per-at-ing"
    more of an exasperation than being "Exasperating"? Why?
2   What makes the speaker sure that "you just *know* he knows he knows"?
    Do you? Why? Does the sloth care if you know he knows he knows?
3   Try reading the poem to convey the idea that the speaker really *is* exas-
    perated with the sloth. Is it possible? Then read it conveying the idea
    that he is charmed by the sloth—and more than a little envious. Easy?
4   Try to figure out a theme (or several) for the poem. Once you have,
    consider whether it (or they) has (have) much to do with what the
    poem means.

[11]   *This Is Just to Say*
             WILLIAM CARLOS WILLIAMS (1883–1963)

I have eaten
the plums
that were in
the icebox

and which   5
you were probably
saving
for breakfast

Forgive me
they were delicious   10
so sweet
and so cold

CONSIDERATIONS

1   What is lost if the title isn't read as an essential part of the poem? Do
    you think that the person who was "probably saving" the plums is
    present as the speaker explains what he has done, or is the speaker writ-
    ing a note about it, perhaps to leave on the kitchen table? Support your
    decision.

2   When do you think it dawned on the speaker that somebody was "probably saving" the plus "for breakfast"—before or after he ate them? How do you know? Is he sorry that he ate them? Or is "sorry" not quite the right word? (Is what he says after "Forgive me" a "reason" for doing what he did, or what?)

3   Do you think that the person who was saving the plums was upset by the fact that they were eaten? Why or why not? Given the kind of explanation the speaker makes, how do you think you would have reacted to his eating your plums and then asking you to forgive him?

4   What personal pronoun dominates the first stanza? the second stanza? What relationship does "Forgive me" in the third stanza bring these two pronouns (and the persons they stand for) into? Could it be argued that the three stanzas are like three scenes composing a short play? What would be the theme of that play?

5   If we had referred to the speaker as "she" instead of "he," would that change your responses to any of the questions?

II

THE POEM
AS A
DRAMATIC SITUATION

EVERY POEM HAS A SPEAKER

i

The most important single factor in a poem considered as a dramatic situation is its speaker. A poem is always spoken by someone—most obviously, by the poet. But when we start looking closely at the dramatic character of poetry, we find that we have to allow for a more immediate speaker than the poet, one whom the poet has imagined speaking the poem, as an actor speaks a part written for him by a playwright. In some instances, this imagined speaker is in no way definite or distinctive; he or she is simply a voice. The speakers of the humorous poems that began this book, with the possible exception of the "Dog" in poem 4, are just this. But often the speaker is much more than a voice, and then whoever it is becomes a contributor to the whole meaning of the poem.

The speaker of "A Man Who Had Fallen Among Thieves" is, for example, somewhat more than a voice. He's obviously not a sentimental fellow given to splashing about in his emotions. He describes the sight before him with clinical attention to vulgar details, and even with a certain superior humor. His humor is directed partly at the victim with his "fifteenthrate" notions of an "emancipated" evening and partly at the "citizens" who (he takes pleasure in reminding us, by the words "graze" and "pastures") are as much sheep as the victim, because their ideas about what is "done" and "not done" are as fifteenthrate as the victim's idea of emancipation. All in all, we'll probably feel that the speaker of the poem is like a hard-boiled newspaperman. He has seen a good deal of the seamy side of things and people, and he's perhaps not above enjoying the shocked look on the faces of the respectable when words like "trouser-fly" and "puke" are poked under their noses. Yet this is the man to whom the experience described in the poem's last stanza happens, and that it does happen to *him* is part of the poem's point. For he's tough-minded enough (as the "citizens" are not) to be able to respond to the life-giving, exalting, almost miraculous experience that arrives when he staggers, with the drunken man in his arms, toward an unknown dimension reaching beyond the stars.

The following poem also has a speaker with a definite personality.

[I]   *The Man He Killed*

THOMAS HARDY (1840–1928)

Had he and I but met
By some old ancient inn,
We should have sat us down to wet
Right many a nipperkin!°

But ranged° as infantry,   5
And staring face to face,
I shot at him as he at me,
And killed him in his place.

I shot him dead because—
Because he was my foe,   10
Just so: my foe of course he was;
That's clear enough; although

He thought he'd 'list,° perhaps
Offhand-like—just as I—

°**nipperkin:** glass holding half a pint.   °**ranged:** set in place.   °**'list:** enlist.

> Was out of work—had sold his traps—°   15
> No other reason why.
>
> Yes; quaint and curious war is!
> You shoot a fellow down
> You'd treat if met where any bar is,
> Or help to half-a-crown.°   20

CONSIDERATIONS

1 What question is the speaker trying to answer in stanza three? What answer does he give? Is it an adequate answer? What in stanzas three and four show that he is not fully satisfied with it?

2 What does his answer have in common with the answer of the man in "Mending Wall" (p. 10) who repeats, "Good fences make good neighbors"? Why would you not expect an answer of this kind from the speaker of "A Man Who Had Fallen Among Thieves"?

3 What words in line 17 suggest there are limitations in the speaker's ability to think and feel deeply about what he has done? How does his way of dismissing the problem throw light on why decent and sensible men keep on going to war?

4 Write a short paper contrasting and showing resemblances among the men who speak in "Dulce et Decorum Est," "A Man Who Had Fallen Among Thieves," and "The Man He Killed." Include evidence from the poems to support your opinions in each case.

°**traps:** belongings (the "tools of his trade").   °**half-a-crown:** a former British coin worth (when the poem was written) about sixty-five cents.

The following two poems have speakers whose personalities are by no means simple as that of the speaker in "The Man He Killed," but there's no doubt about the strongly personal point of view.

[2]   *There Died a Myriad*
                 (Part V of "Hugh Selwyn Mauberley")

                    EZRA POUND (1885–1972)

          There died a myriad,°
          And of the best, among them,
          For an old bitch gone in the teeth,°
          For a botched° civilization.

          Charm, smiling at the good mouth,°   5
          Quick eyes gone under earth's lid,

          For two gross of broken statues,
          For a few thousand battered books.

CONSIDERATIONS

1 What words show the speaker's attitude toward the dead men here? How far does this attitude resemble or differ from the attitude taken by the speaker of the preceding poem toward the man he killed? What kind of person is the speaker?

2 In lines 7–8, the speaker implies that the civilization he's speaking of has little *genuine* respect for art or learning. What words in these lines especially carry this implication?

3 What interests does the speaker of this poem show that would not

---

°**myriad:** a vast number.
°**For an old bitch gone in the teeth:** the connotations of "bitch," old age, and decayed teeth are all suggestive of corruption and degeneration.
°**botched:** messed up, bungled.
°**Charm, smiling at the good mouth:** The dead soldiers were young and pleasant, aid smiled at pretty women.

be apt to concern the speaker in the preceding poem? Does he use any words that the other speaker would be unlikely to use? Which?

4 Would the poem be strengthened or weakened by the omission of line 3? Why? (Consider whether line 4 says the same thing or not.)

5 What would be lost by omitting the word "good" in line 5? (Consider line 3.)

[3]   *The Amish*
            JOHN UPDIKE (1932–   )

The Amish are a surly sect.
They paint their bulging barns with hex
Designs, pronounce a dialect
Of Deutsch,° inbreed, and wink at sex.

They have no use for buttons, tea,   5
Life insurance, cigarettes,
Churches, liquor, Sea & Ski,
Public power, or regrets.

Believing motors undivine,
They bob behind a buggied horse   10
From Paradise to Brandywine,
From Bird-in-Hand to Intercourse.°

They think the Devil drives a car
And wish Jehovah would revoke
The licensed fools who travel far   15
To gaze upon these simple folk.

°**Amish:** a religious sect (Mennonite Christian) stressing simple living.
°**Deutsch:** German (often misleadingly called Dutch, as in Pennsylvania Dutch.
°**Paradise . . . Intercourse:** towns in eastern Pennsylvania (Amish country).

CONSIDERATIONS

1   Why does the speaker call the Amish a "surly sect"? Who thinks so?

2   How can it be argued that "regrets" fits in perfectly with the rest of the items listed in stanza 2?

3   What's a synonym for "undivine"? Why is "undivine" a much more telling word than any synonym for it would be?

4   "Licensed fools" in former times (often kept by kings and often referred to as "court jesters") were so-called because they were given "license," i.e. permission, to speak derisively and insultingly. The moderns who drive to Amish country are "licensed fools" in this sense, says the poem —but in what other sense also (consider the pun in "licensed")?

5   We normally talk of "revoking a license" but in stanza 4 the speaker wants Jehovah (why not "God"?) to "revoke the licensed fools" who travel to Amish country to "gaze." What is gained by the switch? How can people be "revoked"?

6   What kind of person is the speaker? Does he like the Amish? How do you know? Do you, based on what he says? Why or why not?

ii

The following two poems have alternate speakers—a type of "dramatic situation" that very often occurs in poems.

[4]   *Proud Maisie*

SIR WALTER SCOTT (1771–1832)

> Proud Maisie is in the wood,
> Walking so early;
> Sweet Robin sits on the bush
> Singing so rarely.°
>
> "Tell me, thou bonny° bird,   5
> When shall I marry me?"
> "When six braw° gentlemen
> Kirkward° shall carry ye."

°**rarely:** excellently, with rare skill.   °**bonny:** pretty.   °**braw:** well-dressed.   °**Kirkward:** toward the church.

"Who makes the bridal bed,
Birdie, say truly?"   10
"The gray-headed sexton
That delves the grave duly.

The glow-worm o'er grave and stone
Shall light thee steady.
The owl from the steeple sing,   15
'Welcome, proud lady.' "

The speakers in this poem are Proud Maisie and the robin. Proud Maisie is a young girl with love on her mind, as her two questions to the robin show. She is proud with the pardonable pride that comes to all of us in extreme youth, when we seem to carry the future in our pocket like an uncashed blank check. Confident in her beauty, her thoughts turn as inevitably to marriage as the compass needle to the north. There's no shadow of doubt in her mind that the world is all hers. She doesn't ask *whether;* she ask *when* and *with whom.*

The other speaker, Sweet Robin, cannot in fact speak at all, and so makes the best possible speaker for this particular situation. For since his "speech" is not literal, we know that his message is one that Maisie doesn't hear. Maisie's ignorance, of course, is the source of the pity that we feel for her. What comes to Maisie's own ears is simply the robin singing "rarely" in the springtime. What *we* hear, on the other hand, in the robin's song, is a sentence of death. Thus the poem is a dialogue in which neither party actually says anything. Maisie does not "literally" address the robin. The nature of her questions is implicit in her bearing, her youth, her walking in the woods in the spring dawn. Nor does the robin literally reply. His answers are implicit in the world he represents— the world of nature, of which Maisie also is part, and in which the date of execution is unpredictable but the sentence is always death.

By using alternative "speakers," Scott manages to concentrate in a few lines all the feelings of pity and wonder and resignation (since there's nothing that can be done) that we feel when a young man or young woman dies. We are all part of the one nature, his poem seems to say, and the same laws that bear us toward the bridal bed (line 9) bear us also —and perhaps at any instant—to the grave (line 12).

CONSIDERATIONS

1 Compare this poem with "Bredon Hill," which appears on page 12. What lines here correspond in unspoiled joyousness to lines 1–10 of "Bredon Hill"?

2 In "Bredon Hill" our first hint that something may go counter to expectation occurs in line 11. Where does a similar hint first occur in "Proud Maisie"?

3 In "Bredon Hill" the change in the meaning of the bells in lines 26 and 31–35 is acted out for us by changes in the description of their music and in the hearer's attitude to it. What is changed in the last two lines of "Proud Maisie" as compared with what we read in lines 3–4?

[5]   *Piazza Piece*

JOHN CROWE RANSOM (1888–1974)

—I am a gentleman in a dustcoat trying
To make you hear. Your ears are soft and small
And listen to an old man not at all,
They want the young men's whispering and sighing.
But see the roses on your trellis dying   5
And hear the spectral° singing of the moon;
For I must have my lovely lady soon,
I am a gentleman in a dustcoat trying.

—I am a lady young in beauty waiting
Until my truelove comes, and then we kiss.   10
But what gray man among the vines is this
Whose words are dry and faint as in a dream?
Back from my trellis, Sir, before I scream!
I am a lady young in beauty waiting.

°**spectral:** ghostly.

CONSIDERATIONS

1 Who are the two speakers here?

2 In what respects does their dialogue resemble that in "Proud Maisie"? In what respects does it differ? (Consider lines 11–14.)

3 How has the meaning of "trying" in line 1 grown by the time of its reappearance in line 8? How does the meaning of "waiting" in line 9 enlarge by the time of its reappearance in line 14? What happens to the meaning of "dustcoat" by the time we discover who the "gentleman" is?

iii

As the title indicates in the following poem, a single person is speaking inside a monastery. The speaker is a monk, who is revealing his intense hatred of another monk (the Brother Lawrence of line 3) as he watches him working in his garden.

[6]   *Soliloquy of the Spanish Cloister*
               ROBERT BROWNING (1812–1889)

Gr-r-r—there go, my heart's abhorrence!
    Water your damned flowerpots, do!
If hate killed men, Brother Lawrence,
    God's blood, would not mine kill you!
What? your myrtle-bush wants trimming?   5
    Oh, that rose has prior claims—
Needs its leaden vase filled brimming?
    Hell dry you up with its flames!

At the meal we sit together:
    Salve tibi!° I must hear   10
Wise talk of the kind of weather,
    Sort of season, time of year:
Not a plenteous cork-crop: scarcely
    Dare we hope oak-galls, I doubt:
What's the Latin name for "parsley"?   15
    What's the Greek name for Swine's Snout?

°*Salve tibi!* Hail to you!

Whew! We'll have our platter burnished,
    Laid with care on our own shelf!
With a fire-new spoon we're furnished,
    And a goblet for ourself,   20
Rinsed like something sacrificial
    Ere 'tis fit to touch our chaps—°
Marked with *L* for our initial!
    (He-he! There his lily snaps!)

Saint, forsooth! While brown Dolores   25
    Squats outside the Convent bank
With Sanchicha, telling stories,
    Steeping tresses in the tank,°
Blue-black lustrous, thick like horse-hairs,
    —Can't I see his dead eye glow,   30
Bright as 'twere a Barbary corsair's?
    (That is, if he'd let it show!)

When he finishes refection,°
    Knife and fork he never lays
Cross-wise, to my recollection,   35
    As do I, in Jesu's praise.
I the Trinity° illustrate,
    Drinking watered orange-pulp
In three sips the Arian° frustrate;
    While he drains his at one gulp.   40

Oh, those melons! If he's able
    We're to have a feast! so nice!
One goes to the Abbot's table,
    All of us get each a slice.
How go on your flowers? None double?   45
    Not one fruit-sort can you spy?

°**chaps:** jaws.   °**tank:** pool.
°**refection:** meal.
°**Trinity:** unity of God in three persons: Father, Son, and Holy Spirit.
°**Arian:** follower of Arius (died A.D. 336), who denied the Trinity.

Strange!—And I, too, at such trouble
 Keep them close-nipped on the sly!

There's a great text in Galatians,°   7
 Once you trip on it, entails   50
Twenty-nine distinct damnations,
 One sure, if another fails:
If I trip him just a-dying,
 Sure of heaven as sure can be,
Spin him round and send him flying   55
 Off to hell, a Manichee!°

Or, my scrofulous° French novel   8
 On gray paper with blunt type!
Simply glance at it, you grovel
 Hand and foot in Belial's° gripe:°   60
If I double down its pages
 At the woeful sixteenth print,
When he gathers his greengages,°
 Ope a sieve° and slip it in't?

Or, there's Satan! one might venture   9   65
 Pledge one's soul to him, yet leave
Such a flaw in the indenture
 As he'd miss till, past retrieve,
Blasted lay that rose-acacia
 We're so proud of! *Hy, Zy, Hine* . . .°   70
'St, there's Vespers! *Plena gratiâ,*
 Ave, Virgo!° Gr-r-r—you swine!

°**text in Galatians:** In stanza seven the speaker suggests trapping Brother
Lawrence into making heretical statements, thereby damning his soul. St.
Paul's letter to the Galatians is a stinging rebuke to those who would substitute rigid adherence to ritual for the true spirit of Jesus's gospel.
°**Manichee:** The heresy of the Manichee probably referred to here is the
belief that evil is not part of God's creation. A Persian, Manes (A.D. 216?–
276?), founded a religion usually called *Manichaeism.*
°**scrofulous:** diseased; here, pornographic. °**Belial:** one of Satan's hench-
men. °**gripe:** grip. °**greengages:** plums. °**sieve:** meshed basket in
which Brother Lawrence will put the greengages. °***Hy, Zy, Hine:*** probably some sort of Satanic incantation. °***Plena ... Virgo:*** Hail, Virgin,
full of grace (formal prayer).

CONSIDERATIONS

1 In what tone of voice would the speaker say lines 5–7? What different tone would he use for lines 1–4 and line 8?

2 Which of the two tones prevails in stanza three? The platter, shelf, spoons, goblet, and chaps that the speaker mentions are obviously not things he shares with Brother Lawrence; so what does his use of "we" and "our" indicate about his tone of voice here? And also in line 70?

3 What kind of behavior is he ascribing to Brother Lawrence in stanza four? How do we know that it's really the speaker who indulges in such thoughts, rather than Brother Lawrence?

4 Is the speaker's behavior in stanza five particularly praiseworthy, as he obviously thinks it is? What is shown about the speaker by the fact that he finds fault with Brother Lawrence's actions in this regard?

5 Stanza six tells us that the speaker has borne a grudge against Brother Lawrence for a long time. What action does he refer to in lines 45–48? lines 45–48?

6 In stanzas seven, eight, and nine the speaker thinks of three schemes for revenge. One is to trick Lawrence into heresy, and the second into ill desires; the third is to bargain with Satan to destroy Brother Lawrence's favorite shrub. What is revealed about the speaker in these stanzas? For instance, why is it significant that in line 54 he admits that Brother Lawrence is as "sure of heaven as sure can be," and that in line 62 the speaker reveals that he knows exactly where the "woeful" print (illustration) *is*, in *his* "French novel"? What, in particular, does his third scheme indicate about the extent of his jealousy and hatred?

7 Just what is it in Brother Lawrence that the speaker detests? Has he revealed anything about the man that is detestable? How do we know that Brother Lawrence is probably as "sure of heaven as sure can be"? What has the speaker revealed about himself?

THE SPEAKER OF A POEM SPEAKS FROM A PERSONAL SITUATION

i

The personal situation in any poem is whatever the speaker of the poem is reacting to. We can easily illustrate this fact from the poems we have read in the preceding sections. In "Mending Wall" (p. 10) the situation is the springtime walking of the boundary line by two farmers. In "A Man Who Had Fallen Among Thieves" (p. 16), the situation is the disheveled, drunken fellow in the dirt, looked at and then abandoned by the "staunch" and "leal" passersby who live at respectable addresses. In "Proud Maisie" (p. 38) the situation for Maisie is the happy spring morning with its natural suggestions of marriage, and the situation for Sweet Robin is the sight of a young girl, beautiful and doomed. What is the situation for each of the speakers in "Piazza Piece" (p. 40)?

What is the situation for each of the speakers in the following poem?

[1]   *A Kind of Good-bye*

THEODORE SPENCER (1902–1949)

I met an old man near a darkened house,
And he looked in my eyes and spoke of that house,
Said the girl with flame in her voice, in her hair.
"What did he say to you standing there?
What did he say to you, darling, darling?"   5

He said that the house was my own house;
Said the girl with flame in her eyes, in her hair;
That's what he said to me standing there;
That's what he said to me, darling, darling.

He said I'd live all day in that house,   10
He said I'd live all night in that house,
Said the girl with flame in her hands, in her hair;
"And what did you answer him standing there?
What did you answer him, darling, darling?"

I said I hated my darkened house,   15
Said the girl with the flame in her skin, in her hair.
That's what I said to him standing there;
That's what I said to him, darling, darling.

But the old man told me to enter that house;
"You are here; we are ready; come into your house";   20
He told me to enter my darkened house,

Said the girl with flame in her heart, in her hair.
That's what he said to me standing there;
That's what he said to me, darling, darling.

CONSIDERATIONS

1 What is the darkened house? Who is the old man? In "Piazza Piece"
the "gray man" (line 11) is contrasted with "my truelove" (line 10).
Who is contrasted in the same way with the "old man" in "A Kind of
Good-bye"?

2 How, in a sense, does the "flame" gradually devour the girl as the
stanzas progress?

3 What resemblance has this poem to "Bredon Hill"?

What is the situation to which the speaker is reacting in the following
two poems?

[2]   *Porphyria's Lover*

ROBERT BROWNING (1812–1889)

The rain set early in tonight,
　　The sullen wind was soon awake,
It tore the elm-tops down for spite,
　　And did its best to vex the lake;
I listened with heart fit to break;   5
When glided in Porphyria; straight
　　She shut the cold out and the storm,
And kneeled and made the cheerless grate
　　Blaze up, and all the cottage warm;
Which done, she rose and from her form   10
Withdrew the dripping cloak and shawl,
　　And laid her soiled gloves by, untied
Her hat, and let the damp hair fall,
　　And, last, she sat down by my side
And called me. When no voice replied,   15
She put my arm about her waist,
　　And made her smooth white shoulder bare,

And all her yellow hair displaced,
    And, stooping, made my cheek lie there,
And spread, o'er all, her yellow hair,   20
Murmuring how she loved me—she
    Too weak, for all her heart's endeavor,
To set its struggling passion free
    From pride, and vainer ties dissever,
And give herself to me for ever.   25
But passion sometimes would prevail,
    Nor could tonight's gay feast restrain
A sudden thought of one so pale
    For love of her, and all in vain:
So, she was come through wind and rain.   30
Be sure I looked up at her eyes
    Happy and proud; at last I knew
Porphyria worshipped me; surprise
    Made my heart swell, and still it grew
While I debated what to do.   35
That moment she was mine, mine, fair,
    Perfectly pure and good: I found
A thing to do, and all her hair
    In one long yellow string I wound
Three times her little throat around,   40
And strangled her. No pain felt she;
    I am quite sure she felt no pain.
As a shut bud that holds a bee,
    I warily oped her lids: again
Laughed the blue eyes without a strain.   45
And I untightened next the tress
    About her neck; her cheek once more
Blushed bright beneath my burning kiss:
    I propped her head up as before,
Only, this time my shoulder bore   50
Her head, which droops upon it still:
    The smiling rosy little head,
So glad it has its utmost will,
    That all it scorned at once is fled,

And I, its love, am gained instead!   55
Porphyria's love: she guessed not how
    Her darling one wish would be heard.
And thus we sit together now,
    And all night long we have not stirred,
And yet God has not said a word!   60

CONSIDERATIONS

1   What is the personal situation of Porphyria in this poem? Why does
    her lover think her "weak" (line 22)? To what sorts of things does he
    probably refer in "vainer ties" (line 24)? What do you think of her
    from the actions ascribed to her in the poem?

2   What is the personal situation of the speaker? Why does he do what
    he does? Step by step, trace the way in which his state of mind is
    made known to us. What is the effect of lines 58–60?

[3]   *Not Waving but Drowning*
                    STEVIE SMITH (1902–1971)

Nobody heard him, the dead man,
But still he lay moaning:
I was much further out than you thought
And not waving but drowning.

Poor chap, he always loved larking°   5
And now he's dead
It must have been too cold for him his heart gave way,
They said.

Oh, no no no, it was too cold always
(Still the dead one lay moaning)
I was much too far out all my life
And not waving but drowning.

°**larking:** fooling around.

CONSIDERATIONS

1 Why is the "him" of the poem referred to as "the dead man" if "still he lay moaning"? In what sense has he always been treated as if he were dead? Note lines 9 and 11—12. What does "cold" mean in line 7? in line 9?

2 What are the literal and nonliteral meanings of "further out" and "far out" in the poem? Imagine, if you can, the terror that would come over you if you were flailing your arms in panic trying to stay afloat and people on the shore simply waved at you, thinking they were gaily returning your greeting.

3 What kind of people are the "they" of the poem (line 8)? Consider especially such phrases as "Poor chop" and "loved larking," the simplistic explanation in line 7 of what happened to the man, and the fact that they don't hear a thing he says. Why is line 7 so long and line 8 so short? How are they meant to be read?

4 Have you ever felt in such a way that the phrase "not waving but drowning" would accurately characterize how other people would misunderstanding you? When and why?

ii

What is the situation of the speakers in the following four poems? What are they reacting to?

[4]   *Ulysses*

ALFRED, LORD TENNYSON (1809–1892)

It little profits that an idle king,°
By this still hearth, among these barren crags,
Matched with an agèd wife, I mete and dole
Unequal laws unto a savage race,
That hoard, and sleep, and feed, and know not me.   5
I cannot rest from travel. I will drink
Life to the lees. All times I have enjoyed
Greatly, have suffered greatly, both with those
That loved me, and alone; on shore, and when
Through scudding drifts the rainy Hyades°   10

°**idle king:** Ulysses, after the Trojan War and his years of adventure before reaching his home island, Ithaca.
°**Hyades:** star group, supposedly bringer of rain.

Vext the dim sea. I am become a name;
For always roaming with a hungry heart
Much have I seen and known,—cities of men
And manners, climates, councils, governments,
Myself not least, but honored of them all,—   15
And drunk delight of battle with my peers,
Far on the ringing plains of windy Troy.
I am a part of all that I have met;
Yet all experience is an arch where-through
Gleams that untraveled world, whose margin fades   20
Forever and forever when I move.
How dull it is to pause, to make an end,
To rust unburnished, not to shine in use!
As though to breathe were life! Life piled on life
Were all too little, and of one to me   25
Little remains; but every hour is saved
From that eternal silence, something more,
A bringer of new things; and vile it were
For some three suns to store and hoard myself,
And this gray spirit yearning in desire   30
To follow knowledge like a sinking star,
Beyond the utmost bound of human thought.

This is my son, mine own Telemachus,
To whom I leave the scepter and the isle—
Well-loved of me, discerning to fulfill   35
This labor, by slow prudence to make mild
A rugged people, and through soft degrees
Subdue them to the useful and the good.
Most blameless is he, centered in the sphere
Of common duties, decent not to fail   40
In offices of tenderness, and pay
Meet adoration to my household gods,
When I am gone. He works his work, I mine.

There lies the port; the vessel puffs her sail;
There gloom the dark, broad seas. My mariners,   45

Souls that have toiled, and wrought, and thought with me,—
That ever with a frolic welcome took
The thunder and the sunshine, and opposed
Free hearts, free foreheads,—you and I are old;
Old age hath yet his honor and his toil. 50
Death closes all; but something ere the end,
Some work of noble note, may yet be done,
Not unbecoming men that strove with gods.
The lights begin to twinkle from the rocks;
The long day wanes: the slow moon climbs; the deep° 55
Moans round with many voices. Come, my friends.
'Tis not too late to seek a newer world.
Push off, and sitting well in order° smite
The sounding furrows; for my purpose holds
To sail beyond the sunset, and the baths° 60
Of all the western stars, until I die.
It may be that the gulfs will wash us down;
It may be we shall touch the Happy Isles,°
And see the great Achilles,° whom we knew.
Though much is taken, much abides; and though 65
We are not now that strength which in old days
Moved earth and heaven, that which we are, we are,—
One equal temper of heroic hearts,
Made weak by time and fate, but strong in will
To strive, to seek, to find, and not to yield. 70

CONSIDERATIONS

1   What is the situation of the speaker? Why is he an "idle king" now?
    What is it he doesn't like about his situation? What has his past been
    like? What do lines 3–5, 11, 13–15, 22–23, and 39–43 in particular tell
    us about the kind of man he is?

°**deep:** sea.   °**sitting . . . order:** Ulysses's ship is a galley; the oarsmen
sit in rows.   °**baths:** i.e., the seas into which the stars seem to sink.
°**Happy Isles:** Greek heroes' heaven.   °**Achilles:** greatest of the Greek
warriors at Troy.

2 To whom is he speaking? What do the speaker and his audience have in common? What are they doing while he's speaking to them? Why is it suitable that they should set off in the waning of the day?

3 Try to state specifically what attitudes of heart and mind Ulysses is meant to stand for, in the poem.

[5]   *Edward*

ANONYMOUS

"Why dois° your brand° sae drap wi bluid,°
        Edward, Edward,
Why dois your brand sae drap wi bluid,
        And why sae sad gang° yee O?"
"O I hae killed my hauke sae guid,°   5
        Mither, mither,
O I hae killed my hauke sae guid,
        And I had nae mair° bot° hee O."

"Your haukis bluid was nevir sae reid,°
        Edward, Edward,   10
Your haukis bluid was nevir sae reid,
        My deir son I tell thee O."
"O I hae killed my reid-roan steid,
        Mither, mither,
O I hae killed my reid-roan steid,   15
        That erst° was sae fair and frie° O."

"Your steid was auld, and ye hae got mair,
        Edward, Edward,
Your steid was auld, and ye hae got mair,
        Sum other dule ye drie° O."   20
"O I hae killed my fadir deir,
        Mither, mither,

°**dois:** does.   °**brand:** sword.   °**bluid:** blood.   °**gang:** go.   °**guid:** good.
°**mair:** more.   °**bot:** but.   °**reid:** red.   °**erst:** once.   °**frie:** spirited.
°**dule ye drie:** grief you suffer.

O I hae killed my fadir deir,
    Alas, and wae° is mee O!"

"And whatten penance wul° ye drie for that,   25
    Edward, Edward,
And whatten penance wul ye drie for that?
    My deir son, now tell me O."
"Ile set my feit in yonder boat,
    Mither, mither,   30
Ile set my feit in yonder boat,
    And Ile fare ovir the sea O."

"And what wul ye doe wi your towirs and your ha,°
    Edward, Edward?
And what wul ye doe wi your towirs and your ha,   35
    That were sae fair to see O?"
"Ile let thame stand tul they doun fa,
    Mither, mither,
Ile let thame stand tul they doun fa,
    For here nevir mair maun° I bee O."   40

"And what wul ye leive to your bairns° and your wife,
    Edward, Edward?
And what wul ye leive to your bairns and your wife,
    Whan ye gang ovir the sea O?"
"The warldis° room, late them beg thrae° life,   45
    Mither, mither,
The warldis room, late them beg thrae life,
    For thame nevir mair wul I see O."

"And what wul ye leive to your ain° mither deir,
    Edward, Edward?   50
And what wul ye leive to your ain mither deir?
    My deir son, now tell me O."

°**wae:** woe.   °**wul:** will.
°**ha:** hall.   °**maun:** must.   °**bairns:** children.   °**warldis:** world's.
°**thrae:** through.   °**ain:** own.

"The curse of hell frae me sall° ye beir,°
          Mither, mither,
The curse of hell frae me sall ye beir,   55
          Sic° counseils ye gave to me O."

CONSIDERATIONS

1 From what situation does Edward speak? How recently has he done
   the deed? What details are added to our realization of the situation,
   and to his, by the questions in stanzas four, five, and six? How does the
   gradual realization help account for the outburst in stanza seven?

2 From what situation does the mother seemingly speak in the beginning? What clues gradually lead us to wonder if this is the whole
   truth? When do we discover her true situation? When does she discover it? How do we know it was not what she expected?

3 Discuss some of the advantages of using two speakers in this poem.

[6]   *La Belle Dame sans Merci°*
                   JOHN KEATS (1795–1821)

Ah, what can ail thee, wretched wight,°
     Alone and palely loitering;°
The sedge° is withered from the lake,
     And no birds sing.

Ah, what can ail thee, wretched wight,   5
     So haggard and so woebegone?
The squirrel's granary is full,
     And the harvest's done.

I see a lily on thy brow,
     With anguish moist and fever dew;   10
And on thy cheek a fading rose
     Fast withereth too.

°**sall**: shall.   °**beir**: bear.   °**sic**: such.
°**Title**: the beautiful lady without mercy.   °**wight**: creature.   °**loitering**:
moving about aimlessly.   °**sedge**: marsh grass.

I met a lady in the meads
 Full beautiful, a faery's child;
Her hair was long, her foot was light,   15
 And her eyes were wild.

I set her on my pacing steed,
 And nothing else saw all day long;
For sideways would she lean, and sing
 A faery's song.   20

I made a garland for her head,
 And bracelets too, and fragrant zone;°
She looked at me as she did love,
 And made sweet moan.

She found me roots of relish sweet,   25
 And honey wild, and manna dew;°
And sure in language strange she said,
 I love thee true.

She took me to her elfin grot,°
 And there she gazed and sighèd deep,   30
And there I shut her wild sad eyes—
 So kissed to sleep.

And there we slumbered on the moss,
 And there I dreamed, ah woe betide,°
The latest° dream I ever dreamed   35
 On the cold hill side.

°**zone:** sash.
°**honey ... dew:** John the Baptist lived on wild honey in the wilderness; manna is the food that the Israelites received miraculously in their time of trial in the wilderness; together with "roots of relish sweet," the food here ironically seems somehow of an unearthly kind that leaves the "wretched wight" unable to take any normal nourishment (all of which is consistent with the lady's bewitchment).
°**grot:** cave.   °**betide:** befall.   °**latest:** last.

I saw pale kings, and princes too,
    Pale warriors, death-pale were they all;
Who cried—"La belle Dame sans merci
    Hath thee in thrall!" °   40

I saw their starved lips in the gloam
    With horrid warning gapèd wide,
And I awoke, and found me here
    On the cold hill side.

And this is why I sojourn here   45
    Alone and palely loitering,
Though the sedge is withered from the lake,
    And no birds sing.

CONSIDERATIONS

1 Who are the two speakers in the poem? When does the second speaker begin?

2 What is the personal situation out of which the "wretched wight" speaks? What did he hope for from the lady he had met "in the meads"? What did he receive from her? What do the paleness stressed in lines 2, 11, and 37–38 and the "starved lips" of line 41 tell us about the nature of the lady and what she does to her victims? By what wiles did she get the principal speaker "in thrall"? In what sense has he consciously chosen his own doom?

3 How is his personal situation (his spiritual situation, perhaps) underscored by the physical situation in which he is found "loitering"? How is the autumn appropriate to this story, as sunset is to the story of "Ulysses"? Consider what the shortened fourth line of each stanza (basically the ballad form) contributes to the sense of barrenness and lifelessness.

°**thrall:** servitude.

[7]   *Neutral Tones*
                 THOMAS HARDY (1840–1928)

We stood by a pond that winter day,
And the sun was white as though chidden of ° God,
And a few leaves lay on the starving sod;
—They had fallen from an ash, and were gray.

Your eyes on me were as eyes that rove   5
Over tedious riddles solved years ago;
And some words played between us to and fro
    On which lost the more by our love.

The smile on your mouth was the deadest thing
Alive enough to have strength to die;   10
And a grin of bitterness swept thereby
    Like an ominous bird a-wing. ....

Since then, keen lessons that love deceives,
And wrings with wrong, have shaped to me
Your face, and the God-curst sun, and a tree,   15
    And a pond edged with grayish leaves.

CONSIDERATIONS

1 What is the situation of the poem? Is the speaker talking to someone
   directly? If not, why does he (or she) use "your" in the last three
   stanzas?
2 Explain the meaning of the images in stanzas 2 and 3. What are the
   implications of "tedious" (6), "played" (7) and "grin of bitterness"
   (11)?
3 How do lines 15–16 echo lines 1–4? What is gained by this echoing?
4 In what ways are the implications of the title carried out? Consider word
   choice, particularly in stanza 1. How do the images of stanzas 2 and 3
   emphasize "neutralness"? What is an appropriate synonym for "neutral"
   in this context: uninvolved? uncommitted? indifferent? lifeless? In what
   sense is there nothing at all *neutral* about the tone of the poem?

°**chidden of**: rebuked by.

5 How does Hardy, through the extensive use of "and's" in stanzas 1 and 4, reinforce the idea that the dead love affair can be, and constantly is, dredged up from memory? Read the poem giving more than usual emphasis to the "and's" and see what comes out.

6 What are the *keen lessons* to which the speaker refers in stanza 4? In other words, what has the dead love affair come to stand for in his/her life?

THE SPEAKER OF A POEM SPEAKS TO SOME KIND OF AUDIENCE

i

We have used previous poems to illustrate the fact that every poem has a speaker, and we can also use previous poems to illustrate the fact that this speaker is addressing an audience. The only problem is that of deciding whether the audience is a person or persons imagined in the poem (for instance, the person called "darling" in "A Kind of Good-bye") or a group of hearers or readers altogether outside it—in short, *us*. In the same way, as we saw earlier, the speaker may vary from a person imagined in the poem to a "voice" altogether outside it—in short, the poet. In a literal sense, of course, the poet always stands behind any imagined speaker and speaks through him or her, just as we always stand beyond any imagined audience and listen through it.

In the following poem by Robert Herrick (as in "Proud Maisie," "Piazza Piece," "A Kind of Good-bye," "Edward," "La Belle Dame sans Merci," and all other poems with two speakers), there are actually *three* audiences: the rose, the young lady to whom the rose is being sent, and we—the hearers or readers.

[1]   *To the Rose*

ROBERT HERRICK (1591–1674)

Go, happy rose, and interwove
With other flowers, bind my love.
Tell her, too, she must not be
Longer flowing, longer free,
That so oft has fettered° me.   5

———————————

°**fettered:** bound, tied up.

Say, if she's fretful, I have bands
Of pearl and gold, to bind her hands;
   Tell her, if she struggle still,
   I have myrtle° rods, at will,
   For to tame, though not to kill.   10

Take thou my blessing thus, and go,
And tell her this—but do not so,
   Lest a handsome anger fly
   Like a lightning from her eye,
   And burn thee up, as well as I.   15

CONSIDERATIONS

1 What are the "bands of pearl and gold" in lines 6–7? What are the "rods" in line 9? How fearsome a rod would myrtle make?

2 What does the speaker gain by pretending to address the rose and letting the lady overhear? Why will she be pleased that he calls the rose "happy" (line 1)? What is the resemblance between this poem and Pope's "Epigram" (p. 6)?

3 Why does the speaker change his mind in line 12? Or does he?

4 Behind this poem lies the custom of sending an ambassador with instructions. How does this custom heighten the compliment involved?

ii

Consider the question of audience(s) in the following four poems.

[2]   *Song, To Celia*

BEN JONSON (1572–1637)

Drink to me only with thine eyes,
   And I will pledge with mine;
   Or leave a kiss but in the cup,

°**myrtle:** a flowering vine sacred to Venus, goddess of love.

And I'll not look for wine.
The thirst that from the soul doth rise   5
    Doth ask a drink divine;
But might I of Jove's nectar sup,
    I would not change for thine.

I sent thee late a rosy wreath,
    Not so much honoring thee,   10
As giving it a hope that there
    It could not withered be.
But thou thereon didst only breathe,
    And sent'st it back to me,
Since when it grows and smells, I swear,   15
    Not of itself, but thee.

CONSIDERATIONS

1 This poem is a series of compliments addressed to an audience of one.
   The basis of these compliments in the first stanza is the action of drinking healths. Who are the drinkers in this instance? What in fact are
   they drinking besides wine? What compliment is paid to the lady in
   lines 1–4? In lines 5–8? In what sense can the first stanza be considered
   an expanding compliment?

2 What is the basis of the compliment in the second stanza? In what
   sense is the second stanza even more complimentary to the lady than
   the first one is?

3 What response do you suppose the speaker hopes for from his audience
   of one?

[3]   *Holy Sonnet 14*

JOHN DONNE (1572–1631)

Batter my heart, three-personed God; for you
As yet but knock, breathe, shine, and seek to mend.
That I may rise and stand, o'erthrow me and bend
Your force to break, blow, burn, and make me new.
I, like an usurped town, to another due,   5

Labor to admit you, but, oh, to no end;
Reason, your viceroy in me, me should defend,
But is captived and proves weak or untrue.

Yet dearly I love you and would be lovèd fain,
But am betrothed unto your enemy: 10
Divorce me, untie or break that knot again,
Take me to you, imprison me, for I,
Except you enthrall me, never shall be free,
Nor ever chaste, except you ravish me.

CONSIDERATIONS

1 To what does the speaker compare himself and to what does he
   compare God in lines 1–4? in lines 5–8? in lines 9–14? How are these
   metaphors related? In other words, what manner of action is common
   to all of them? Would it make any difference if they were introduced
   in any other order? Explain.

2 The prayer is filled with what seem to be contradictions—e.g. "That
   I may rise and stand, o'erthrow me" (line 3). Find at least two more
   such contradictions in lines 12–14. Is there a similar contradiction in
   the very idea of asking God to use force on us? Why will God's force
   be necessary? (Consider who the *usurper* is in line 5 and who the
   enemy is in line 10.)

3 A well-known Christian prayer, speaking of God, ends: "Whose
   service is perfect freedom." How can *service* be *freedom?* How does
   this contradiction relate to those in Donne's poem?

4 Write a paragraph arguing that the speaker really addresses his poem
   to two audiences: (a) God (b) himself.

[4]   *To a Mouse*

On Turning Her Up in Her Nest with the Plough, November, 1785

ROBERT BURNS (1759–1796)

    Wee, sleekit,° cowrin, tim'rous beastie,
    O, what a panic's in thy breastie!
    Thou need na start awa sae° hasty,
             Wi' bickering° brattle!°
    I wad be laith° to rin an' chase thee,   5
             Wi' murd'ring pattle!°

    I'm truly sorry Man's dominion
    Has broken Nature's social union,
    An' justifies that ill opinion
             Which makes thee startle   10
    At me, thy poor, earth-born companion,
             An' fellow-mortal!

    I doubt na, whyles,° but thou may thieve.
    What then? poor beastie, thou maun° live!
    A daimen° icker° in a thrave°   15
             'S a sma' request.
    I'll get a blessin wi' the lave,°
             And never miss't!

    Thy wee bit housie, too, in ruin!
    Its silly wa's° the win's are strewin!   20
    An' naething, now, to big° a new ane,
             O' foggage° green!
    An' bleak December's winds ensuin,
             Baith snell ° and keen!

°**sleekit:** sleek.   °**sae:** so.   °**bickering:** scurrying.   °**brattle:** clatter.
°**laith:** loath.   °**pattle:** an instrument for pushing chunks of dirt, etc., off
the plow.   °**whyles:** on occasion.   °**maun:** must.   °**daimen:** occasional.
°**icker:** ear of corn.   °**thrave:** twenty-four sheaves.   °**lave:** rest.   °**wa's:**
walls.   °**big:** build.   °**foggage:** moss.   °**snell:** piercing.

Thou saw the fields laid bare an' waste,   25
An' weary Winter comin fast,
An' cozie here, beneath the blast,
                    Thou thought to dwell,
Till crash! the cruel coulter° past
                    Out thro' thy cell.   30

That wee bit heap o' leaves an' stibble,°
Has cost thee mony a weary nibble!
Now thou's turned out, for a' thy trouble,
                    But° house or hald,°
To thole° the Winter's sleety dribble,   35
                    An' cranreuch° cauld!

But, Mousie, thou are no thy lane,°
In proving foresight may be vain:
The best-laid schemes o' Mice an' Men,
                    Gang aft a-gley,°   40
An' lea'e us nought but grief and pain,
                    For promised joy.
Still thou art blest, compared wi' me!
The present only toucheth thee;
But, Och! I backward cast my e'e,°   45
                    On prospects drear!
An' forward, tho' I canna see,
                    I guess an' fear!

CONSIDERATIONS

1 Who is addressing the mouse and under what circumstances? What is
   his attitude toward the mouse? How do you know?

2 Stanzas seven and eight put the incident in a larger context than the
   details of the first six stanzas have suggested. What is the shift in

---

°**coulter**: the cutter on the plow.   °**stibble**: stubble.   °**But**: without.
°**hald**: hold, protecting shelter.   °**thole**: bear.   °**cranreuch**:
hoarfrost.   °**no thy lane**: not alone.   °**Gang aft a-gley**: go oft awry.
°**e'e**: eye.

audience, despite the fact that the speaker is still addressing the mouse? What relevance have the first six stanzas to this shift?

3 What is the advantage of pretending to say everything directly to the mouse? (Retell the incident in your own words as if you were the speaker telling it, not to the mouse but to a friend.)

[5]   *I'm Nobody. Who Are You?*
                   EMILY DICKINSON (1820–1886)

> I'm nobody. Who are you?
> Are you nobody too?
> Then there's a pair of us.
> Don't tell—they'd banish us, you know.
>
> How dreary to be somebody,   5
> How public—like a frog—
> To tell your name the livelong June
> To an admiring bog.

CONSIDERATIONS

1 What has to be the answer to the question in the second line? Why? Read the first two lines aloud several times. Is there any way you can read them so as to suggest that the response might be "no"?

2 Who are the "they" of line 4? How do you know? Why would "they" banish "nobodies"?

3 In what sense is a frog "public"? How can it be said that he "tells his name"? What's a bog to a frog? What else is a bog in this poem?

4 Would anything be lost if "the livelong June" were changed to read "the whole of June"? If so, what?

5 Why would anybody rather be a "nobody" than a "somebody"? Would you (even if your answer to line 2 was yes)? Does the speaker *really* think she's (he's) nobody? If you know that you're nobody, and if you prefer things that way, are you really nobody?

EVERY POEM IS CHARACTERIZED BY A DISTINCTIVE TONE

i

The tone of a poem, like its meaning, is the consequence of all its elements sounding together like matched bells. But the most important single influence on tone is the speaker's consciousness of the situation and the audience. Let's look again at Herrick's poem on page 58. Its *speaker* is obviously a lover—any young lover; his character beyond this remains largely undefined. The speaker's *situation* is the love affair with the young lady, who, though she has long captivated the lover (line 5), has not become his captive in turn. Now he will make a strong plea—accompanied by the gift of a garland to "bind" her—that she consent to become bound in love to him. The speaker's *audiences* are, as we have noticed already, the rose in the garland, the young lady, and we. How shall we estimate the tone?

A first clue to the tone is revealed in the first two lines. The speaker sends this flowery garland in order that his love may see that bonds are not to be feared; and he calls the rose "happy" (line 1) because as part of the garland it will have the luck to embrace and bind her, as he would like to do. There is, in short, a marked youthful tenderness in the tone with which the speaker meets his situation and his audience. But along with the tenderness go other attitudes and feelings, just as other flowers accompany the rose. His suggestion about taming her with "rods" of myrtle is a bit of comic whimsy, a little joke. Rods made out of myrtle would actually be only vinelike tendrils, which would never hurt, though they might, like the garland, bind. The handcuffs made of pearl and gold are also a piece of whimsy: what the speaker means is bridal rings and bracelets. The last stanza summarizes all aspects of the poem's tone. We have its tenderness in "Take thou my blessing thus, and go"; the comic whimsy in the mock fear of being burned to death by the "lightning" of her eye; and under it all, since the fear is not *entirely* mock, the lover's zeal to win at last the love for which he longs.

Following is a passage of dialogue from Shakespeare's play *Romeo and Juliet*. It represents the moment of the lovers' first meeting, when both are struck with love at first sight, at an evening masquerade ball in Juliet's home. Romeo, dressed as a "palmer"—a pilgrim to a holy shrine—proceeds to address Juliet as if she were a saint whose shrine he has at last reached; and she, taking the cue, replies in the same way. By line 14 he has kissed her, and by line 18 he has kissed her again. The variations of tone in the lovers' speech as they progress to their first embrace (almost as in a dream) are worth close examination.

[1]   From *Romeo and Juliet,* I, v

WILLIAM SHAKESPEARE (1564–1616)

ROMEO   If I profane with my unworthiest hand
        This holy shrine, the gentle sin is this,
        My lips, two blushing pilgrims, ready stand
        To smooth that rough touch with a tender kiss.

JULIET Good pilgrim, you do wrong your hand too much,   5
        Which mannerly devotion shows in this;
        For saints have hands that pilgrims' hands do touch,
        And palm to palm is holy palmers' kiss.

ROMEO   Have not saints lips, and holy palmers too?

JULIET Ay, pilgrim, lips that they must use in prayer.   10

ROMEO   O, then, dear saint, let lips do what hands do;
        They pray; grant thou, lest faith turn to despair.

JULIET Saints do not move,° though grant for prayers' sake.

ROMEO   Then move not, while my prayer's effect I take.
        Thus from my lips by thine my sin is purged.   15

JULIET Then have my lips the sin that they have took.

ROMEO   Sin from my lips? O trespass sweetly urged!
        Give me my sin again.

CONSIDERATIONS

1   In what way does the tone of the Shakespearean passage resemble that
    of "To the Rose"? Are there any differences? How do you think the
    tone of the Shakespearean passage is affected by the presence of two
    speakers?

2   What does the pilgrim–saint situation contribute to the tone?

3   Why do the pilgrim-lips blush? Because the shrine has been profaned?
    Because they are the color that all lips are? Because of the proposal
    they are now making? Or all three? Explain.

4   What differing senses does "devotion" (line 6) have here? Consider it
    first as a religious term and then as a lover's. What about "faith" (line
    12)? "Despair" (line 12)? "Sin" (lines 2, 15, 16, 17, 18)? What does
    Juliet mean by "move" in line 13? What does Romeo mean by it in
    line 14?

°**move:** begin, make the first move.

In Robert Browning's "In a Gondola," there's another scene between lovers. In this scene, however, there's only one speaker.

[2]   From *In a Gondola*

ROBERT BROWNING (1812–1898)

The moth's kiss first!
Kiss me as if you made believe
You were not sure, this eve,
How my face, your flower, had pursed
Its petals up; so, here and there   5
You brush it, till I grow more aware
Who wants me, and wide ope I burst.

The bee's kiss, now!
Kiss me as if you entered gay
My heart at some noonday,   10
A bud that dares not disallow
The claim, so all is rendered up.
And passively its shattered cup
Over your head to sleep I bow.

CONSIDERATIONS

1 Who speaks in the passage from "In a Gondola"—lady or man? In what situation? (For instance, would you say they had just met?) With what tone?

2 How would you distinguish the tone of this poem from that of "To the Rose"? From that of the Shakespearean passage?

Compare the following poem carefully with the passage from *Romeo and Juliet.*

[3]   *The Nun*

JAMES HENRY LEIGH HUNT (1784–1859)

If you become a nun, dear,
A friar I will be;
In any cell you run, dear,
Pray look behind for me.
The roses all turn pale, too;   5
The doves all take the veil, too;
The blind will see the show:
What! you become a nun, my dear!
I'll not believe it, no.
If you become a nun, dear,   10
The bishop love will be;
The cupids every one, dear,
Will chant, "We trust in thee":
The incense will go sighing,
The candles fall a-dying,   15
The water turn to wine:
What! you go take the vows, my dear!
You may—but they'll be mine.

CONSIDERATIONS

1 What kind of man would you say the speaker of this poem is? What
evidence do you find that he is unpleasantly sure of himself? How do
lines 3–4 indicate that he has a childish view of the life led by friars
and nuns?

2 Lines 5–7 say that a lot of other "miracles" will as soon take place as
the miracle of his dear's becoming a nun. What are these other miracles? What are they in stanza two?

3 Do the terms adopted from religion have the same effect on tone in
this poem as in the Shakespearean passage? Which poem shows more
respect for religious terms? Are there any religious references in the
Shakespearean passage that make you uncomfortable? Are there in
"The Nun"?

ii

Here are nine more poems on which to try your ear for tone. Consider in each case the speaker(s), the situation, the audience(s), and, in general, the language.

[4] *Apparently with No Surprise*

EMILY DICKINSON (1830–1886)

Apparently with no surprise
To any happy flower,
The frost beheads it at its play
In accidental power.

The blond assassin passes on,   5
The sun proceeds unmoved
To measure off another day
For an approving God.

[5] *"Out, Out—"*

ROBERT FROST (1874–1963)

The buzz-saw snarled and rattled in the yard
And made dust and dropped stove-length sticks of wood,
Sweet-scented stuff when the breeze drew across it.
And from there those that lifted eyes could count
Five mountain ranges one behind the other   5
Under the sunset far into Vermont.
And the saw snarled and rattled, snarled and rattled,
As it ran light, or had to bear a load.
And nothing happened: day was all but done.
Call it a day, I wish they might have said   10
To please the boy by giving him the half hour
That a boy counts so much when saved from work.
His sister stood beside them in her apron
To tell them "Supper." At the word, the saw,
As if to prove saws knew what supper meant,   15

Leaped out at the boy's hand, or seemed to leap—
He must have given the hand. However it was,
Neither refused the meeting. But the hand!
The boy's first outcry was a rueful laugh,
As he swung toward them holding up the hand   20
Half in appeal, but half as if to keep
The life from spilling. Then the boy saw all—
Since he was old enough to know, big boy
Doing a man's work, though a child at heart—
He saw all spoiled. "Don't let him cut my hand off—   25
The doctor, when he comes. Don't let him, sister!"
So. But the hand was gone already.
The doctor put him in the dark of ether.
He lay and puffed his lips out with his breath.
And then—the watcher at his pulse took fright.   30
No one believed. They listened at his heart.
Little—less—nothing! and that ended it.
No more to build on there. And they, since they
Were not the one dead, turned to their affairs.

[6]   From *Macbeth*, V, v

           WILLIAM SHAKESPEARE (1564–1616)

        She should have died hereafter;
    There would have been a time for such a word.
    Tomorrow, and tomorrow, and tomorrow,
    Creeps in this petty pace from day to day,
    To the last syllable of recorded time;   5
    And all our yesterdays have lighted fools
    The way to dusty death. Out, out, brief candle!
    Life's but a walking shadow, a poor player
    That struts and frets his hour upon the stage
    And then is heard no more. It is a tale   10
    Told by an idiot, full of sound and fury,
    Signifying nothing.

CONSIDERATIONS

1 The three selections (4, 5, and 6) you have just read have a theme in common. What is it?

2 The third selection is spoken by Shakespeare's Macbeth when his hold on the throne of Scotland, which (with the encouragement of his wife) he has murdered his king to obtain, is threatened on all sides by the enemies his crimes have made for him. Now, in addition, the news of his wife's death is brought to him. How does this knowledge affect our understanding of the tone of the passage; in other words, in view of the situation what would you have expected the tone to be? Remorseful? Defiant? What is it actually?

3 To what phrase in the passage from Shakespeare does the title of poem 5 refer? How does our recognition of this allusion to *Macbeth* affect our understanding of the meaning of "Out, Out—"? Does it warn us not to take "Out, Out—" as the verdict of Robert Frost on life?

4 Which two of these selections have the most in common as to tone? Which two have the least? How do you know?

5 In what way does the theme of "Apparently with No Surprise" resemble the theme of "Proud Maisie" (p. 38)? What *additional* problem does it raise (consider the references to "accidental power," to the sun proceeding "unmoved," and to "an approving God")? Where is the same problem raised in "Out, Out—" and the *Macbeth* passage?

[7]   *Channel Firing*

THOMAS HARDY (1840–1928)

That night your great guns, unawares,
Shook all our coffins as we lay,
And broke the chancel window-squares,
We thought it was the Judgment-day

And sat upright. While drearisome   5
Arose the howl of wakened hounds:
The mouse let fall the altar-crumb,
The worms drew back into the mounds,

The glebe cow° drooled. Till God called, "No;
It's gunnery practice out at sea   10
Just as before you went below;
The world is as it used to be:

"All nations striving strong to make
Red war yet redder. Mad as hatters°
They do no more for Christés° sake   15
Than you who are helpless in such matters.

"That this is not the judgment-hour
For some of them's a blessed thing,
For if it were they'd have to scour
Hell's floor for so much threatening . . .   20

"Ha, ha. It will be warmer when
I blow the trumpet (if indeed
I ever do; for you are men,
And rest eternal sorely need)."

So down we lay again. "I wonder,   25
Will the world ever saner be,"
Said one, "than when He sent us under
In our indifferent century!"

And many a skeleton shook his head.
"Instead of preaching forty year,"   30
My neighbor Parson Thirdly said,
"I wish I had stuck to pipes and beer."

°**glebe cow:** *glebe* refers to land belonging to a parish church; the cow also
belongs to the church.
°**Mad as hatters:** a common expression that means "completely zany."
°**Cristés:** Middle English spelling; along with later references to ancient
Britain, it suggests the timelessness of warlike behavior.

Again the guns disturbed the hour,
Roaring their readiness to avenge,
As far inland as Stourton Tower,°   35
And Camelot,° and starlit Stonehenge.°

CONSIDERATIONS

1   The poem was written in 1914, on the eve of the First World War.
    The Channel referred to is the English Channel between England and
    France. Who is being addressed in line 1? Who is speaking? What has
    disturbed the speaker? Who else responds to the noise of the "great
    guns," and what kind of responses are made?

2   What kind of answer does God give to the speaker's question about
    "Judgment-day"? What is the tone of His answer? How is it consis-
    tent with the rather casual, even whimsical, behavior of the coffin-
    dwellers before and after He speaks? The subject matter of the poem
    is the ages-long eagerness of humanity to make "red war yet redder."
    What is significant about the fact that such a serious indictment of
    human behavior is made in such a lighthearted, joking way?

3   In what ways does the tone shift in the last stanza? Why are Camelot,
    Stourton Tower, and Stonehenge referred to?

[8]   *Mr. Flood's Party*

            EDWIN ARLINGTON ROBINSON (1869–1935)

Old Eben Flood, climbing alone one night
Over the hill between the town below
And the forsaken upland hermitage
That held as much as he should ever know
On earth again of home, paused warily.   5
The road was his with not a native near;
And Eben, having leisure, said aloud,
For no man else in Tilbury Town to hear:

°**Stourton Tower:** a tower in Wiltshire, England, commemorating King
Alfred's successes against Danish invaders in the ninth century.
°**Camelot:** King Arthur's castle and court.
°**Stonehenge:** ancient ruins on Salisbury Plain in England.

"Well, Mr. Flood, we have the harvest moon
Again, and we may not have many more;   10
The bird is on the wing, the poet says,
And you and I have said it here before.
Drink to the bird." He raised up to the light
The jug that he had gone so far to fill,
And answered huskily: "Well, Mr. Flood,   15
Since you propose it, I believe I will."
Alone, as if enduring to the end
A valiant armor of scarred hopes outworn,
He stood there in the middle of the road
Like Roland's ghost winding a silent horn.°   20
Below him, in the town among the trees,
Where friends of other days had honored him,
A phantom salutation of the dead
Rang thinly till old Eben's eyes were dim.

Then, as a mother lays her sleeping child   25
Down tenderly, fearing it may awake,
He set the jug down slowly at his feet
With trembling care, knowing that most things break;
And only when assured that on firm earth
It stood, as the uncertain lives of men   30
Assuredly did not, he paced away,
And with his hand extended paused again:

"Well, Mr. Flood, we have not met like this
In a long time; and many a change has come
To both of us, I fear, since last it was   35
We had a drop together. Welcome home!"
Convivially returning with himself,
Again he raised the jug up to the light;
And with an acquiescent quaver said:
"Well, Mr. Flood, if you insist, I might.   40

°**Like . . . horn:** Roland is the hero of the medieval French *Song of Roland:*
a man who holds the Spanish passes against the invading Moslems till one
by one his men are killed and at last he himself—but not before he has
succeeded in alerting the army of Charlemagne by successive blasts on his
great horn.

"Only a very little, Mr. Flood—
For auld lang syne. No more, sir; that will do."
So, for the time, apparently it did,
And Eben evidently thought so too;
For soon amid the silver loneliness   45
Of night he lifted up his voice and sang,
Secure, with only two moons listening,
Until the whole harmonious landscape rang—

"For auld lang syne." The weary throat gave out,
The last word wavered; and the song being done,   50
He raised again the jug regretfully
And shook his head, and was again alone.
There was not much that was ahead of him,
And there was nothing in the town below—
Where strangers would have shut the many doors   55
That many friends had opened long ago.

CONSIDERATIONS

The situation is simple enough. An old man has outlived his time: lines
55–56 tell us that his friends are all dead. His "party" must be with himself, the jug his only companion. He realizes only too well that "most
things break" (line 28) and that he is "enduring to the end/A valiant
armor of scarred hopes outworn" (lines 17–18). Such a man could be the
object of scorn, or derision, or disgust, or pity. Old Eben Flood (what is
his name meant to suggest?) comes through the poem as none of these.
There is no minimizing of his aloneness, but that aloneness has something
of dignity and self-respect in it.

1 Characterize the way Mr. Flood speaks to and answers himself. Is
   there any self-pity in him? What kind of men might pledge toasts to
   each other in just this way?

2 What feelings about Mr. Flood do the reference to Roland and his
   horn call up, here? In what respects is his situation at all like Roland's?
   In what respects is it not? In what way is his jug like a horn?

3 Is the comparison in lines 25–28 a ridiculous one in this context, or has
   it been prepared for? (Consider line 14 and the fact that he's already
   answering himself "huskily.")

4 What action is suggested in lines 31–32 and 36–37? How does it give an added sense of tenderness to his "party"? How do "For auld lang syne" and the "two moons listening" reinforce that sense?

5 Define the tone of the poem.

[9]   *My Papa's Waltz*
              THEODORE ROETHKE (1908–1963)

The whiskey on your breath
Could make a small boy dizzy;
But I hung on like death:
Such waltzing was not easy.

We romped until the pans   5
Slid from the kitchen shelf;
My mother's countenance
Could not unfrown itself.

The hand that held my wrist
Was battered on one knuckle;   10
At every step I missed
My right ear scraped a buckle.

You beat time on my head
With a palm caked hard by dirt,
Then waltzed me off to bed   15
Still clinging to your shirt.

CONSIDERATIONS

1 Is the speaker a young boy or a grown man recalling an incident (or repeated incidents) from childhood? Explain. Who is the audience? Are there several audiences? Explain.

2 Exactly what is being described? Why is the man "waltzing" his son? What do lines 3 and 16 tell us about the son's reaction to the "waltz"? But what does "romped" (line 5) tell us?

3 Explain lines 7–8. Why didn't the mother interfere?

4 The small boy was clearly terrified by the drunken dance. But what is the grown man's reaction? Consider the title. Consider, too, the use of "waltzing," "romped," and such a line as "Could not unfrown itself." How would the implications of the latter differ if it read "Still kept an icy frown"? In short, how does the tone qualify the sense of terror remembered?

[10]   *Damn Her*

JOHN CIARDI (1916–   )

Of all her appalling virtues, none
leaves more crumbs in my bed, nor
more gravel in my tub
than the hunch of her patience
    at its mouseholes.   5

She would, I swear, outwait
the Sphinx in its homemade quandaries
once any scratching in the walls
has given her to suspect
    an emergence.   10

It's all in the mind, we say. With her
it's all in the crouch, the waiting
and the doing indistinguishable. Once
she hunches to execution, time is merely
    the handle of the switch: 15

she grasps it and stands by for whatever
will come, certainly, to her sizzling
justice. Then, inevitably always daintily
she closes her total gesture
    swiftly disdainfully as   20

a glutton tosses off a third dozen
oysters—making light of them—as if
his gluttony were a joke that all
may share. (The flaps and bellies
    of his grossness   25

are waiting, after all, for something
much more substantial than
appetizers.)—"Bring on the lamb!" her look
says over my empty shells. "Bring on
  the body and the blood!"   30

[II]   *Coup de Grâce*

              A. D. HOPE (1907–   )

Just at the moment the Wolf,
Shag jaws and slavering grin,
Steps from the property wood,
O, what a gorge, what a gulf
Opens to gobble her in,   5
Little Red Riding Hood!

O, what a face full of fangs!
Eyes like saucers at least
Roll to seduce and beguile.
Miss, with her dimples and bangs,   10
Thinks him a handsome beast;
Flashes the Riding Hood Smile;

Stands her ground like a queen,
Velvet red of the rose
Framing each little milk-tooth,   15
Pink tongue peeping between.
Then, wider than anyone knows,
Opens her minikin mouth

Swallows up Wolf in a trice;
Tail going down gives a flick,   20
Caught as she closes her jaws.
Bows, all sugar and spice.
O, what a lady-like trick!
O, what a round of applause!

QUESTIONS

1   Each of these poems pays tribute to a woman. What *is* this tribute?
   How does manipulation of *tone* prevent the tribute from becoming
   mawkish or sentimental? By what devices is the tone manipulated—
   allusions? comparisons? word choice? verse form?

2   Which tribute do you prefer? Why? Do you find the word "tribute"
   objectionable in this case? Why or why not?

[12]   *Chorus*
                      JOHN CIARDI (1916–   )

They were singing Old MacDonald in the schoolbus
With a *peep peep* here and a *peep peep* there after
Margie Littenach had been delivered to the right mailbox
And the gears had gnashed their teeth uphill to the Cliff House
Where the driver, shifting gears, honked at the countergirls,   5
And the tourists turned from panorama all smiles
To remember schooldays, long curls, hooky, and how
The view had always stretched for miles and miles
Where the gentle cumulus puffed small in gentle weather
Putting a cottonfluff roof on the green world leaning   10
      down hill
To the bluelevelfield of sea, and all together
With an *oink oink* here and a *moo moo* there the children
Were singing Old MacDonald in the schoolbus
When a bolt fell from the compound interest problem,
A rod broke in the third chapter of the Civicsbook   15
Where the county had no money for inspection in the
      first place
                              and
Momentum had no brakes, but with a *honk honk* here
And a *honk honk* there went sidewise over tirescreech
Downturning in round air away from panorama where   20
Even the tourists could tell sea didn't measure each
Stone falling, or button, or bolt, or Caroline Helmhold,
Nor anywhere its multitudinous self incarnadine, but
      only swallowed

What books, belts, lunchpails, pity
Spilled over the touristfaredge of the world and Old   25
    MacDonald

CONSIDERATIONS

1 There's no end punctuation in the poem, even at the end. Is there any place where a period would normally go except at the end? If this is just one long sentence, why do you suppose the poet chose to make it so? Why no period at the end?

2 What connection has the song "Old MacDonald" got with what the poem is about and the unending way it's constructed?

3 Explain the meaning of:
   a. "a bolt fell from the compound interest problem" (What did "money" have to do with it?)
   b. "a rod broke in the third chapter of the Civicsbook" (What did violation of good government have to do with it?)
   c. "went sidewise over tirescreech" (What do you take to be the subject of "went"?)
   d. "its multitudinous self incarnadine" (*Incarnadine* is a verb here, *sea* is its subject, *self* its object, In Shakespeare's *Macbeth*, the hero, looking at his bloody hands after he has murdered a sleeping man with his dagger, despairs of ever being able to wash them clean; even the whole ocean, he feels, cannot wash away *this* blood; rather the blood will "the multitudinous seas incarnadine," i.e. stain the sea red. Does knowing this about the phrase add something to its value here? What?)

III

THE POEM

AS A

PATTERN OF

RHYTHM AND SOUND

RHYTHM

i

All of the aspects of poetry that we've been dealing with thus far apply as well to literature in prose, although with different emphases. The two aspects we come to now also have relevance to prose, but it's in this area of rhythm and sound that the greatest difference lies between poetry and prose. In a rough kind of way, anyone who has looked at poetry on a page or who has read some of it aloud is aware that it looks different and reads differently: it has some kind of definite line and stanza pattern, and some kind of patterned rhythm or melody.

Line and stanza pattern are obviously peculiar to poetry. Rhythm is *not*. Everything we say in daily speech has rhythm. In English this rhythm is dependent mainly on the fact that certain words or syllables get a heavier stress than do other words or syllables in the stream of speech, that there are definite rises and falls as the voice moves along, and that definite kinds of pauses cut up the sound stream, as the following examples roughly illustrate:

doll
You need two   ar
               s.

Heaviest stress on *doll;* pitch rises on *doll,* then falls and fades, signaling "end of statement."

                    , ars?   Heaviest stress on *doll;* pitch rises on *doll,* con-
                doll   tinues to rise, and fades, signaling "question,
You need two   please answer."

one, two, three, four, fi   After each number there is a slight rise in pitch
                        v   but no voice fade, until the last when pitch falls
                            e   and voice fades, signaling "end of count."

        Smi   Division indicated by commas in print is signaled
            t   in speech by stress and pitch change and voice
Mr.   h, my next door   not fading.
neigh   Yank
        bor, likes the   ee
                            s.

In this discussion we'll confine ourselves to stress.[1] Stress is what we
hear as loudness or emphasis of a word or syllable in relation to surrounding words or syllables. One-syllable words spoken in isolation—as in the
preceding group of numbers or in a list—get what sounds to our ears like
equally heavy stress:

> **one, two, three, in, hit, walk, four, so, went, five**

In words of two syllables spoken in isolation, one of the syllables gets a
heavier stress than the other:

> **un**der, **for**ward, be**fore**, **sis**ter, ar**range**, **in**stant, un**til**

In most two-syllable words, the syllable that doesn't get heavy stress is
sounded weakly, as in the words just cited. But in some two-syllable
words, the weaker syllable still gets prominence:

> **white**wash, **black**board, **green**house, **moon**lit, **fore**tell

The important point is that the stress is never entirely equal in these cases:
the stress on one of the syllables is always slightly heavier. Try pronounc-
ing the foregoing words with major stress on the syllables that aren't in

---

[1] What we will say about speech rhythms will be, of necessity, very sketchy. A de-
tailed analysis would have to deal with many other considerations besides stress, but
a look at how stress operates gives an adequate introduction to the poet's special way
of handling the patterns of language. The discussion is dependent on several suggestions in John Thompson's Introduction to his *The Founding of English Metre* (New
York: Columbia University Press, 1961), which, as he says, relies heavily on *An Out-
line of English Structure,* by George L. Trager and Henry Lee Smith, Jr. (Norman,
Okla.: Battenburg Press, 1951).

boldface to see what is meant about unequal stress. Also compare the following pairs to see that there's a decided difference in the amount of stress given to the weaker syllables:

> whitewash–whiter
> blackboard–blackness
> greenhouse–greenest
> moonlit–moonlet

In words of more than two syllables, only one of the syllables takes primary or heaviest stress:

benefit, holiday, recovery, transportation, tobacco, intercept, independence, anniversary, constitutional

But differing degrees of weaker stress are likely to fall on the other syllables. For instance, the heaviest stress of "holiday" is on *hol*, but the last syllable, *day*, receives more stress than does the middle syllable, *i*. Similarly, in the last three words listed above, the first syllable doesn't get primary stress, but gets heavier stress than do the other weak syllables.

In summary, single-syllable words spoken in isolation get definite stress. In two-syllable words, one of the syllables gets major stress and the other gets either almost no stress or an obvious stress weaker than the major one. In words of more than two syllables, one syllable gets primary stress, and the others get almost none or stresses weaker than the primary one. For practice in identifying stress within words, mark the stresses of the following, using (′) for heavy stress, (`) for obvious stress that isn't heaviest, and (˘) for weak stress:

fort	accommodate	suburb
wigwam	Stonewall	suburban
Sunday	automatically	foolhardy
formal	sundown	canyon
uniform	approach	beginning
denounce	wishes	sublet
rapid	wishywashy	apprentice
fundamental	capital	icebound

ii

When words are grouped into phrases, the patterns of heavier and weaker stress depend on the makeup of the word group. For instance, in the phrase "my first anniversary," the heaviest stress normally comes on *ver* (the stressed syllable of the noun that the other words modify), as it does if we pronounce the word in isolation. But if the group is expanded to "my first anniversary party," the heaviest stress normally comes on the first syllable of "party." In the phrase "one small stone," the heaviest stress comes on "stone" if the phrase is spoken normally. (If we deviate from the normal to put heaviest stress on "small," we do it to emphasize a distinction between a small stone and another kind of stone, presumably a larger one. If we deviate from the normal to put the heaviest stress on "one," we do it to emphasize the fact that we're talking about one stone and no more.) If we add the word "house" to the group and get "one small stone house," the heaviest stress now automatically falls on "house," unless, again, we want to make some special distinction.

iii

Three important observations may now be made. First, as is shown by the shift of heaviest stress to "party" when the word is added to the phrase "my first anniversary" and by the shift of heavier stress to "house" when it is added to "one small stone," heaviest stress in English tends to fall at the end of a word group when the group is spoken normally. Notice the following examples:[1]

a small picket

a small picket fence

a small picket fence gate

running around

running around town

running around Town Hall

---

[1] Most language scholars agree that there are three possible degrees of stress when words are spoken in isolation and four when words are grouped together. Thus, in "my first anniversary party," *par* normally gets heaviest stress, but *first* and *ver* get heavier stress than *my* and *an*, which in turn get heavier stress than the weak-stressed syllables in "anniversary" and "party." It's not easy, without a great deal of training, to decide which of the two medium stresses is present in a given word group. For our purposes, it will be sufficient to distinguish only three degrees of stress within word groups. We'll use the symbols designated on page 83.

ăt hĭs báck

ăt hĭs bàck dóor

ăt hĭs bàck dòor wĭndŏw

The bóy / sànk thrée.

The smàll bóy / sànk thrèe shíps.

The smàll bòy píratĕ / sànk thrèe shìps éasĭlў.

Second, some classes of words automatically get weaker or stronger stress because of what they are. Any *preposition* ("in," "on," "with"), any *noun marker* ("a," "an," "the," "every"), any *auxiliary* ("is," "will be," "has been," plus a verb), most *pronouns* ("he," "his," "it"), and any simple *conjunction* ("and," "but," "so") normally get weak stress. Nouns in their normal positions usually get primary stress: subject—"The *boy* is awake"; direct object—"We buried the *cat*"; and object of preposition—"on the *beach*." Modifiers that precede the word they modify normally get medium stress:

smàll grèen búsh

crùmblĭng stòne wáll

quĭet antĭcĭpátĭon

quíetlў thínkĭng

Predicate adjectives ("She seemed *sick*"; "He's *healthy*") and adverbs in final sentence position ("He caught the ball *easily*"; "Your check came *through*") normally take primary stress. Verbs as predicates seldom get heaviest stress, unless they appear at the end of a sentence:

Hĕ càlled thĕ dóg.

The sún sànk dŏwn ĭn thĕ wést.

Wĕ sàt quíetlў.

Thèy léft.

Third, what these two facts about English mean in practice is that we may have an extraordinary variety of speech rhythms in ordinary, everyday word groups. We encounter groups in which every word receives some appreciable stress:

> old gray stone wall
>
> sank coal crates there
>
> Please leave coats here.
>
> Young dogs bark loud.

We encounter groups in which weakly stressed and strongly stressed words and syllables alternate to make remarkably regular patterns:

> the house of stone in Bangor, Maine
>
> my friend who thinks he's Cary Grant
>
> All of the hoods will be whooping it up in the spring.

We even encounter groups whose patterns of regularity are so prolonged that they can be turned into a crude form of versification with minimal effort. Consider the following sentence quoted from *The Founding of English Metre*, mentioned earlier: "What metre adds to language is precisely the element of imitation that makes of the two, when they are joined, the art of verse." If we eliminate the words "the element of" and emphasize the particular phrasing we want by printing the passage in lines, we get a clumsy stanza:

> What metre adds to language is
> Precisely imitation,
> That makes of the two, when they are joined,
> The art of vers[ification].

The result is far from poetry, but it shows how easily speech patterns may be directed toward the regularities and semiregularities that we call the meters of verse.

iv

Poets are people who pay attention to the facts about speech that we've been discussing and make it their business to arrange words so that their speech rhythms will accomplish something. The two things normally accomplished are (1) the heightening of pleasure—because we all enjoy rhythm—and (2) the heightening or clarification of meaning. Let's look at an instance of the latter first, in a short poem titled "The Span of Life":

> The old dog barks backward without getting up.
> I can remember when he was a pup.
>
> *—The Span of Life*
> ROBERT FROST (1874–1963)

In this short poem, the old dog is contrasted with the pup he once was. The words of the first line describe his behavior now; the words of the second line, notably the word "pup," refer to him as he was then. This contrast in what the lines say is paralleled in the respective rhythms. The first line contains relatively heavy stresses bunched together:

The old dog barks backward without getting up.

Speaking playfully, we might say that the line, like the dog, refuses to get up off its haunches and move. Speaking more exactly, we can at least say that the line is heavy and halting in a way that suits the idea of an old dog not wanting to get up. The second line, on the other hand, has a swift, light, and fairly regular movement:

I can remember when he was a pup.

Its movement is lively—like the pup's, we might say if speaking playfully, but at any rate lively in a manner that fits the idea of a capering young dog. And here there's a further point to notice. Though some sort of contrasting relation is established between the old dog and the young one by what the words say, we don't know precisely what the contrast is until we pay attention to the rhythm. So far as the words are concerned, the point might be that the old dog is no longer so good a watchdog as he was. It's the contrast in the rhythms that helps direct our attention to the differing movements of the two ages of dog, and so helps us to understand that the young one is all curiosity, barking at everything it sees, and rushing to see everything it barks at, while the old one, having been through all this, simply turns his head and *barks backward*.

CONSIDERATIONS

Where in the following passages would you say that rhythm *most clearly* heightens or clarifies meaning?

1 Here's a Greek warrior at the siege of Troy struggling to hurl a great
boulder against his Trojan enemies:

> When Ajax strives some rock's vast weight to throw,
> The line too labors, and the words move slow.
>
> —From *An Essay on Criticism*
> ALEXANDER POPE (1688–1744)

2 Here's a thirsty man in a desert, longing for water. (The cicada he
speaks of is the grasshopper locust.)

> If there were the sound of water only
> Not the cicada
> And dry grass singing
> But sound of water over a rock
> Where the hermit-thrush sings in the pine trees   5
> Drip drop drip drop drop drop drop
> But there is no water
>
> —From *The Waste Land,* V
> T. S. ELIOT (1888–1965)

3 Here's a complete poem called "Reflections on Ice-Breaking":

> Candy
> Is dandy
> But liquor
> Is quicker.
>
> —*Reflections on Ice-Breaking*
> OGDEN NASH (1902–1971)

To appreciate the part played by rhythm in the previous example,
notice what rephrasing the poem does:

> In my experience I have found that candy
> For purposes of social ice-breaking is dandy,
> But if I had to choose, I think I'd choose liquor,
> As being on the whole and in most circumstances quicker.

4 Here's a knight in his armor ("harness") clambering among rocks in
a mighty effort to reach a lake before the wounded man he carries on
his back dies:

Dry clashed his harness in the icy caves
And barren chasms, and all to left and right
The bare black cliff clanged round him, as he based
His feet on juts of slippery crag that rang
Sharp-smitten with the dint of armèd heels—   5
And on a sudden, lo! the level lake,
And the long glories of the winter moon.

—From *Morte d'Arthur*
ALFRED, LORD TENNYSON (1809–1892)

5 Here's a description of a crowded three-lane expressway at the height
   of the evening rush hour, the lanes of traffic moving at high speed:

Evening traffic homeward burns,
Swift and even on the turns,
Drifting weight in triple rows,
Fixed relation and repose.
This one edges out and by,   5
Inch by inch with steady eye.
But should error be increased,
Mass and moment are released;
Matter loosens, flooding blind,
Levels driver to its kind.   10

—From *Before Disaster*
YVOR WINTERS (1900–1968)

6 Here's a story of a man who gets hanged just as the poem, titled
   "Eight O'Clock," ends. How does the language of the last two lines imitate the actions of the clock before striking and the action of the trap
   door through which the condemned man plunges?

He stood, and heard the steeple
    Sprinkle the quarters on the morning town.
One, two, three, four, to market place and people
    It tossed them down.

Strapped, noosed, nighing his hour,   5
    He stood and counted them and cursed his luck.
And then the clock collected in the tower
    Its strength, and struck.

—*Eight O'Clock*
A. E. HOUSMAN (1859–1936)

What would be lost if the second stanza were as follows?

> Unable to move, awaiting his time,
>> He stood and counted them and cursed his luck.
> Then, in the tower, the clock did chime,
>> Sealing his doom when it struck.

7   Here's a poem about a decision. The finality of decision is hammered home by line length and rhythm. Notice the abrupt second and fourth lines of the first two stanzas and the even more abrupt second and fourth lines in the last stanza, giving the effect of firmness and fixity.

> The soul selects her own society,
> Then shuts the door;
> On her divine majority
> Obtrude no more.
>
> Unmoved, she notes the chariot's pausing   5
> At her low gate;
> Unmoved, an emperor is kneeling
> Upon her mat.
>
> I've known her from an ample nation
> Choose one;   10
> Then close the valves of her attention
> Like stone.
>
>> —*The Soul Selects Her Own Society*
>> EMILY DICKINSON (1830–1886)

METER

i

From the preceding examples we can see that rhythm may support and clarify meaning. But rhythm may also please for its own sake, and the principle that accounts for the pleasure it gives is the principle of recurrence with change.

Our lives are rooted in things that recur: the four seasons, day and night, our three meals a day, work and relaxation, breathing, blinking, and a thousand more. We find something secure and satisfying in old friends, old tunes, old slippers, old scenes. At the same time, however, we long for variety. We like to see new faces as well as old ones, eat new foods in new places, move through a variety of responsibilities in our jobs. Many of the things that especially delight us therefore are those in which a strong element of recurrence is balanced by a strong element of change. From this combination comes much of the appeal of music and dancing (for these are built of stated themes and fixed steps opening out into variations and improvisations)—and the appeal of poetry.

Regular rhythmic recurrence in poetry is called *meter*. The recurrence is essentially a stress recurrence, or, more accurately, a "weak-stress–strong-stress" recurrence. The normal stress pattern of speech is fitted into a two-stress metrical pattern, having (in most English poetry) the major stress second. In the examples, we'll use *o* to mark *metric* weak stresses and *s* to mark metric strong stresses to keep clear the distinction between *metrical* stress patterns and *speech* stress patterns.

$$\overset{o}{\text{weak-}}\overset{s}{\text{strong,}} \ \overset{o}{\text{weak-}}\overset{s}{\text{strong,}} \ \overset{o}{\text{weak-}}\overset{s}{\text{strong}}$$

or

$$\overset{o}{\text{ta-}}\overset{s}{\text{tum,}} \ \overset{o}{\text{ta-}}\overset{s}{\text{tum,}} \ \overset{o}{\text{ta-}}\overset{s}{\text{tum}}$$

or

$$\overset{o}{\text{to}} \ \overset{s}{\text{barn}} \ \text{and} \ \overset{o}{\text{stack}} \ \text{and} \ \overset{s}{\text{tree}}$$

When the speech stresses are subjected to the two-stress metrical pattern, primary speech stresses generally remain strong and weak speech stresses generally remain weak. Medium speech stresses become metric strongs or metric weaks depending on the surrounding stresses; between strong or medium stresses they become metric weaks, and between weak stresses they become metric strongs. Also, weak speech stresses sometimes become strong metric stresses when they come between two weak speech stresses that are also weak metric stresses. Thus in any given line of verse, single-syllable words can have stresses not normally received in speech. Obviously, however, the unstressed syllables of multisyllable words cannot take strong metric stresses if the result would be an incorrect pronunciation of the word. Likewise, insistence on giving equal emphasis to all strong metric stresses in defiance of normal speech rhythms creates distortion.

A few examples will make clear what we've been saying. Let's look at the first stanza of "The Man He Killed" (p. 34), marked first with normal speech stresses:

Had he and I but met

By some old ancient inn,

We should have sat us down to wet

Right many a nipperkin!

The first line clearly indicates the weak-strong pattern in normal speech and sets the metrical pattern by which the second line is read. As is clear, the "metric-weak–metric-strong" movement suggested in the first line accommodates the language of the second line very effectively. The normally weak-stressed "by" and the normal pronunciation of "ancient inn" provide the framework; "old" gets weak metric stress coming between the relative strongs on "some" and the first syllable of "ancient." If, however, the words "In the dark alley near the warehouse" followed "Had he and I but met," the potential pattern established in the first six words would be effectively annulled, and we would probably ignore the regularity of the first line. Even when the substitute second line is printed in verse form, it doesn't give us a suggestion of metric regularity:

> Had he and I but met
> In the dark alley near the warehouse . . .

On the other hand, in Hardy's lines printed as prose the regularity remains:

> Had he and I but met by some old ancient inn . . .

The third line of the stanza fits smoothly, with the established metrical pattern hinting a strong on "should" and a weak on "we." The speech rhythm of the last line also fits the metrical pattern, with the almost unnoticeable addition of two weak stresses in a row: "many a." (But we may see how effective the slight break in the established pattern is by contrasting the present line with the more metrically regular "So many nipperkins!")

Now let's mark the second stanza of Hardy's poem with metric strongs and weaks instead of speech rhythm stresses.

> o   s   o s o s
> But ranged as infantry,
> o   s o   s   o s
> And staring face to face,
> o s o s o s o s
> I shot at him as he at me,
> o   s   o   s o   s
> And killed him in his place.

The strong metric stresses and the strong speech stresses match almost perfectly, the only marked deviation coming in the last line where the weak speech stress on "in" gets strong metric stress, coming as it does between two weak speech stresses. This is not to say that "in" should be given much more emphasis than it would normally have in speech. To emphasize it results in an unnatural singsong. On the other hand, the listener or reader must be aware that the metrical stress falls where it does, and the line should not be read as if it were part of a prose sentence, such as, "When he reappeared near the battered tank, I took careful aim and killed him in his place."

ii

We have noted previously that the "weak-strong" metric pattern is dominant in English poetry. This metric pattern is called *iambic,* and its individual units are called *iambs,* or sometimes (since a basic unit of measurement in English meter is the *foot,* formed in this case of one weak stress and one strong stress) *iambic feet.* Almost every poem we have looked at thus far is in the iambic pattern. Here are some examples. Read them aloud—but remember that when a weak speech stress and a strong metric stress, or a strong speech stress and a weak metric stress, fall on the same syllable or word, the speech stresses are only slightly modified: the weak speech stress in a strong metric position will take a very *little* more emphasis than it would normally have, and the strong speech stress in a weak metric position will take a very *little* less emphasis.

     s   o   o s o   s o s   o s
Something there is that doesn't love a wall,
     o   s   o s o   s   o s
That sends the frozen-ground-swell under it,
     o   s   o s o   s   o s   o s
And spills the upper boulders in the sun; . . .

—From Mending Wall

     o   s   o s   s   o s o   s
Cliff Klingenhagen had me in to dine
     o   s   o s   o s o   s   o   s
With him one day; and after soup and meat,
     o   s   o s o   s   o   s o s
And all the other things there were to eat, . . .

—From Cliff Klingenhagen

     o s   o s   o   s o
In summertime on Bredon
        o   s   o   s   o s
The bells they sound so clear; . . .

—From Bredon Hill

```
    s    o    o    s    o    s    o    s
Brushing from whom the stiffened puke
o   s   o    s o s   o    s
i put him all into my arms
    o    s    o    s    o    s    o    s
and staggered banged with terror through
o   s   o    s o    s   o    s
a million billion trillion stars.
```

—From *A Man Who Had Fallen Among Thieves*

```
    o    s    o s o s o    s
A sweet disorder in the dress
s    o    o    s    o    s    o    s
Kindles in clothes a wantonness; . . .
```

—From *Delight in Disorder*

```
    o    s   o    s o    s    o    s
A narrow fellow in the grass
o    s   o s o   s
Occasionally rides;
o   s   o    s    o    s   o    s
You may have met him,—did you not?
o   s   o    s   o   s
His notice sudden is.
```

—From *A Narrow Fellow in the Grass*

This iambic (weak-strong) meter dominates English poetry because it's a regularization of the basic rhythmic pattern of the language itself. English sentences are built as a series of word groups; and, as we've seen, the stress pattern of the word group is essentially weak-strong, since the primary stress almost always comes at the end of the group. The imposed iambic meter is thus a "model of the larger units of the language"[1] itself, or as the quotation used earlier puts it: "What metre adds to language is precisely the element of imitation that makes of the two, when they are joined, the art of verse."[2] We have, therefore, in any line of verse two separate rhythmic considerations to combine into a third:

1. The two-stress metrical pattern.
2. The normal speech rhythm stress.
3. The actual product of these two in any given line.

---

[1] John Thompson, *The Founding of English Metre* (New York: Columbia University Press, 1961), p. 12.

[2] *Ibid.*, p. 9.

Since there are always weak and strong stresses at work in metered
English poetry, there can be other ways of ordering them than the iambic
pattern. It's simplest, and also most accurate, to think of these other patterns as variations on the iambic, and that's how we'll treat them here.
The most obvious variation comes from reversing the iamb to produce a
"strong-weak" meter. The individual unit, or foot, is called in this case a
trochee, and the over-all pattern or meter is called *trochaic*. Here's a good
specimen of it in a stanza from Tennyson's "The Lady of Shalott":

    s   o   s   o   s   o   s   o
    Willows whiten, aspens quiver,
    s o   s   o   s   o   s   o
    Little breezes dusk and shiver
    s   o   s   o   s   o s o
    Through the wave that runs forever
    s   o s   o   s   o   s o
    By the island in the river
                s   o   s   o   s   o s
                Flowing down to Camelot.   5
    s   o   s   o   s   o   s   o
    Four gray walls, and four gray towers,
    s o   s   o   s   o   s   o
    Overlook a space of flowers,

    s   o   s o   s   o   s   o
    And the silent isle imbowers
              o   s o s   o   s
              The Lady of Shalott.

Very few poems in English are written in this consistently trochaic
meter. Many, however, are written with four strong metric stresses in each
line, with one of the strongs at the beginning and one at the end, as in
the following:

    s   o   s o   s   o   s
    Evening traffic homeward burns,
    s   o s o   s   o   s
    Swift and even on the turns,
    s   o   s   o s o   s
    Drifting weight in triple rows,
    s   o s o   s   o s
    Fixed relation and repose.

                    —From *Before Disaster*
                    YVOR WINTERS (1900–   )

    s   o   s   o s o   s
    Earth, receive an honored guest;
    s   o   s   o s   o   s
    William Yeats is laid to rest:

 s o s o s o s
Let the Irish vessel lie

 s o s o s o s
Emptied of its poetry.

       —From *In Memory of W. B. Yeats*
        w. h. AUDEN (1907–1973)

  s o s o s o s
Tiger, Tiger, burning bright

 s o s o s o s
In the forests of the night,

  s o s o s o s
What immortal hand or eye

 o s o s o s   o s
Could frame thy fearful symmetry?

        —From *The Tiger*
       WILLIAM BLAKE (1757–1827)

Such meters are best looked on as essentially iambic despite the strong opening stresses in each line. We might, of course, regard them as imperfectly trochaic—but notice the damage done by the weak final syllable when we recast into perfect trochaic:

  s o   s o s   o s o
Evening traffic homeward burning,
Swift and even on the turning,
Drifting weight in go condition,
Fixed in triple-laned position.

  s   o   o s o   s o
Earth, receive an honored patron;
William Yeats has changed his matron:
See the Irish vessel lying
Emptied of its versifying.

  s o   s o   s o   s o
Tiger, Tiger, burning brightly
In the forest darkness nightly.

There's much less damage when we recast, instead, to supply the weak first syllable of perfect iambic:

  o s   o   s o   s   o   s
As evening traffic homeward burns,
It's swift and even on the turns,
All drifting weight in triple rows,
In fixed relation and repose.

Sweet Earth, receive an honored guest;
Our William Yeats is laid to rest:
O let the Irish vessel lie
Now emptied of its poetry.

O Tiger, Tiger, burning bright
In all the forests of the night.

Opening and closing with a strong stress, the original lines have maximum weight for their length.

A second major variation on iambic is the *anapest* or *anapestic foot,* a pattern of two metrically unstressed words or syllables followed by a stressed one. This foot is essentially an iamb with an extra metric weak inserted before the metric strong:

With a leap and a bound the swift anapests throng.

SAMUEL TAYLOR COLERIDGE (1772–1834)

As a sloop with a sweep of immaculate wings on her delicate spine
And a keel as steel as a root that holds in the sea as she leans,

—From *Buick*
KARL SHAPIRO (1913–   )

"Oh where are you going?" said reader to rider,
"The valley is fatal when furnaces burn,
Yonder's the midden whose odors will madden,
That gap is the grave where the tall return."

—From *O Where Are You Going?*
W. H. AUDEN (1907–1973)

I sprang to the stirrup, and Joris, and he;
I galloped, Dirck galloped, we galloped all three;
"Good speed!" cried the watch, as the gatebolts undrew;
"Speed!" echoed the wall to us galloping through;

—From *How They Brought the Good News from Ghent to Aix*
ROBERT BROWNING (1812–1889)

It's obvious from the examples given that a poem dominated by anapestic meter in English has a "leap and a bound," as Coleridge says, or at least a sense of swift movement that is not congenial to very many subjects. The same observation is true of the third variation, the *dactyl*. This is a strong metric stress followed by two weak metric stresses —in other words, a trochee with an extra metric weak inserted after the metric strong, as in the following:

s   o o s o o
Take her up tenderly,

s   o o s
Lift her with care,

s   o o s o o
Fashioned so slenderly,

s   o o s
Young, and so fair!

—From *The Bridge of Sighs*
THOMAS HOOD (1799–1845)

Though they occur with some frequency as variations within iambic lines, both anapestic and dactylic meters have very limited use in English. As we've noted, they're used as basic meters mainly for special subjects, as in Shapiro's "Buick." The fact is that any *sustained* deviations from iambic meter call attention to themselves so pointedly (with exceptions that we'll discuss later) that under most circumstances the deviations would put undue emphasis on form at the expense of meaning.

One other kind of metrical variation should be mentioned: the recurrence of several strong-stressed syllables in a row. Since regular speech rhythms must receive their due in poetry, there are bound to be cases where several such stresses succeed each other, as we saw in "The Span of Life" (p. 87). The following examples illustrate gradations of this kind of variation. The first three contain obviously strong stresses with definite pauses between them; the second three have stress strong enough to override the regular meter and therefore to slow down the movement of the line considerably; the third three get definite speech rhythm stress, but not enough to force strong metric stress:

> **Blow, blow,** ye wintry winds . . .

> **Break, break, break,**
>   On thy cold gray stones, O sea! . . .

> **Out, out,** brief candle . . .

> When Ajax strives some **rock's vast weight** to throw . . .

The apparition of these faces in the crowd:
Petals on a **wet, black bough.**

The old **dog barks back**ward without getting up, . . .

By **some old ancient** inn. . . .

And Camelot, and **starlit Stonehenge.**

Mine, O thou lord of life, **send my roots rain.**

iii

We come back now to the way in which speech stress and metrical stress come together to form poetic rhythm—the actual rhythm of the verse line. Left to itself with no counterforce against it, regular metrical recurrence, even with occasional substitution of the kind we've just looked at, would produce results like this:

She SHOULD have DIED here AF ter;
There WOULD have BEEN a TIME for SUCH a WORD.
To MOR row, AND to MOR row, AND to MOR row,
Creeps IN this PET ty PACE from DAY to DAY,
To THE last SYL la BLE of re COR ded TIME;   5
And ALL our YES ter DAYS have LIGHT ed FOOLS
The WAY to DUST y DEATH. Out, OUT, brief CAN dle!
Life's BUT a WALK ing SHAD ow, A poor PLAY er
That STRUTS and FRETS his HOUR up ON the STAGE
And THEN is HEARD no MORE. It IS a TALE   10
Told BY an ID iot, FULL of SOUND and FU ry,
Sig NIF (y)ing NOTH ing.

—From *Macbeth*, V, v
WILLIAM SHAKESPEARE (1564–1616)

But speech rhythm supplies that counterforce, creating in the line a sort of tug-of-war, or tension, that brings pleasure to the tongue and ear. If we read the *Macbeth* passage, taking account of its speech rhythms as well as its meter, we get:

She should have died here af ter;

There would have been a time for such a word.

To mor row, and to mor row, and to mor row,

Creeps in this pet ty pace from day to day,

To the last syl la ble of re cor ded time;   5

And all our yes ter days have light ed fools

The way to dust y death. Out, out, brief can dle!

Life's but a walk ing shad ow, a poor play er

That struts and frets his hour u pon the stage

And then is heard no more. It is a tale   10

Told by an id iot, full of sound and fur y,

Sig ni fy ing noth ing.

Read in this way the varying speech rhythms pull against the implied fixed meter, but are never allowed to destroy it. Just the opposite, in fact: a more than usual divergence from regularity, as in lines 7–8, is likely to be compensated by a more than usual regularity, as in lines 9–10.

Now notice how in E. A. Robinson's "Cliff Klingenhagen" the speech stresses of the first three lines match almost perfectly the metrical stresses, primarily because the weak-stressed words and syllables match the weak metric stresses. Then, in the fourth line come four definite speech stresses in a row that slow down the smooth flow of the first three lines and in a sense "act out" the deliberateness with which Cliff Klingenhagen serves the wine and wormwood. The metrical stress is marked above the speech stress.

o   s   o   s   o   s   o   s   o   s
Cliff Klingenhagen had me in to dine

o   s   o   s   o   s o   s   o   s
With him one day; and after soup and meat,

o   s   o   s o   s   o   s   o   s
And all the other things there were to eat,

o   s   o   s   o
Cliff took two glasses . . .

For further illustration of the rhythmic variation that the marriage of metrical pattern and speech rhythm produces, look at the following first lines of poems, all of which are in the same metrical pattern (five iambs to each line):

Cliff Klingenhagen had me in to dine . . .

When I see birches bend to left and right . . .

When I have fears that I may cease to be . . .

Thou art indeed just, Lord, if I contend . . .

To be, or not to be—that is the question . . .

Avenge, O Lord, thy slaughtered saints, whose bones . . .

Five years have passed; five summers, with the length . . .

There was a time when meadow, grove, and stream . . .

The same kind of wide variation may be seen in the following lines, all of which are iambic with four strong poetic stresses:

It is an ancient mariner . . .

She walks in beauty, like the night . . .

Earth, receive an honored guest . . .

Stern Daughter of the Voice of God . . ˒

Behold her, single in the field . . .

Mock on, mock on, Voltaire, Rousseau . . .

Love seeketh not itself to please . . .

The morning comes to consciousness . . .

To summarize, poetic rhythm combines regularity with irregularity. Regularity most often is the result of some definite underlying meter. Irregularity comes mainly from normal speech rhythms. There's no hard and fast line between the two. When we have speech rhythms free from any obvious pattern of recurrence, we have prose. When we have unrelieved regularity of metrical pattern, we have a singsong. Pleasurable poetic rhythms remain far removed from either extreme.

iv

We can now look at other factors that have a great deal to do with determining regularity and irregularity in a poem: line length, stanza pattern, and the speech sounds themselves.

Line length is a matter of the number of individual units, or feet, that succeed each other in the line. It's not impossible to have lines of one foot or even six feet, but these are rare in English verse. Most lines have three feet (trimeter), four feet (tetrameter), or five feet (pentameter).

Stanza pattern is determined by the length of the line and the patterning of the rhyme scheme. A stanza like those in Emily Dickinson's "Apparently with No Surprise" (p. 69) contains alternate lines of four feet and three—usually represented for brevity's sake as 4, 3, 4, 3. Its rhymes (if we accept the "eye-rhyme" of the second stanza) occur at the end of the second and fourth lines in each stanza—usually represented as a, b, c, b. A stanza like that of Leigh Hunt's "The Nun" (p. 68) has lines of three feet, except for line 8, which has four. This pattern is represented 3, 3, 3, 3, 3, 3, 3, 4, 3. Its rhymes link the first and third lines, the second and fourth lines, the fifth and sixth lines, and the seventh and ninth lines; the eighth line is unrhymed. This pattern is represented a, b, a, b, c, c, d, e, d.

The following passages give you a chance to test your ability to recognize line lengths and stanza patterns. Read the passages aloud and then answer the questions at the close.

[1]   From *King Richard II*, III, ii
                    WILLIAM SHAKESPEARE (1564–1616)

For God's sake, let us sit upon the ground
And tell sad stories of the death of kings:
How some have been deposed; some slain in war;
Some haunted by the ghosts they have deposed;
Some poisoned by their wives; some sleeping killed;   5
All murdered:

[2]   From *To His Coy Mistress*
                    ANDREW MARVELL (1621–1678)

But at my back I always hear
Time's wingèd chariot hurrying near.

[3] From *Elegy Written in a Country Churchyard*
THOMAS GRAY (1716–1771)

The curfew tolls the knell of parting day,
The lowing herd wind slowly o'er the lea,
The plowman homeward plods his weary way,
And leaves the world to darkness and to me.

[4] From *She Dwelt Among the Untrodden Ways*
WILLIAM WORDSWORTH (1770–1850)

She dwelt among the untrodden ways
    Beside the springs of Dove,
A maid whom there were none to praise,
    And very few to love.

[5] From *Antony and Cleopatra,* IV, xiv
WILLIAM SHAKESPEARE (1564–1616)

I, that with my sword
Quartered the world, and o'er green Neptune's back
With ships made cities, condemn myself to lack
The courage of a woman; less noble mind
Than she which by her death our Caesar tells,   5
"I am conqueror of myself."

[6] From *Satire III*
JOHN DONNE (1572–1631)

On a huge hill,
Cragged, and steep, Truth stands, and he that will
Reach her, about must, and about must go;
And what the hill's suddenness resists, win so.

[7]

From *To Autumn*

JOHN KEATS (1795–1821)

Season of mists and mellow fruitfulness,
  Close bosom-friend of the maturing sun;
Conspiring with him how to load and bless
  With fruit the vines that round the thatch-eaves run.

[8]

From *The Wild Swans at Coole*

WILLIAM BUTLER YEATS (1865–1939)

The trees are in their autumn beauty,
The woodland paths are dry,
Under the October twilight the water
Mirrors a still sky;
Upon the brimming water among the stones   5
Are nine-and-fifty swans.

[9]

From *My Papa's Waltz*

THEODORE ROETHKE (1908–1963)

The whiskey on your breath
Could make a small boy dizzy;
But I held on like death:
Such waltzing was not easy.

[10]

From *Preludes*

T. S. ELIOT (1888–1965)

The morning comes to consciousness
Of faint stale smells of beer
From the sawdust-trampled street
With all its muddy feet that press

To early coffee-stands.   5
With the other masquerades
That time resumes,
One thinks of all the hands
That are raising dingy shades
In a thousand furnished rooms.   10

CONSIDERATIONS

1   Which of these passages would you put toward the end of the spectrum where speech rhythms run most completely parallel to meter? Which toward the end where regular meter is most submerged by speech rhythms? Which more or less in the middle?

2   Represent the line lengths in each passage and the rhyme scheme of each that has one.

3   Indicate the places in each of the selections where the basic iambic meter has been replaced by a variation. Give particular attention to the questions below:

a. In passage 2 how does the variation in the second line match the line's movement to its meaning? Consider as an alternative:

> Time's wingèd carriage hasting near.

b. In passage 5 what is the effect of the heavy stress at the beginning of line 2 (with the vowel sound of "sword" repeated)? Consider the alternative:

> I, that with my sword
> Have fourthed the world . . .

In the same passage, what would be lost if the last two lines read:

> Than she which by her death our Caesar tells
> That she is master of herself.

c. In passage 6 how does the rhythm support the meaning of the lines? What is the effect of ending the second line on "will"? Would the word get stress otherwise? Why should it? What is gained by repeating "about must"? How does "must" get prominence? Why should it? What does "suddenness" mean in this context? How is "suddenness" emphasized? What is the purpose of setting the last two short words off as they are? Which word gets heaviest stress? Perhaps a revision will throw light on the original by comparison:

> On a mighty hill,
> Ragged and steep, dwells Truth, and he
> That will reach her, about must go,
> And what the hill's surprise resists, win so.

What is lost in the revision?

d. In passage 10 what is the effect of the extra foot in line 4? (The reader expects a three-foot line, especially when she reaches "feet" to rhyme with "street," but she's made to go on to "press.") How does this extra foot emphasize "press" and why does Eliot want it emphasized? The speech stresses and the metric stresses of the last three lines are almost identical, the only difference being that line 8 begins with one unstressed word, while 9 and 10 begin with two. Mark the speech stresses of the last three lines. How does the repeated pattern match the meaning of the lines? ("Hands" are "raising . . . shades" in a "thousand . . . rooms.")

V

Two other kinds of rhythm patterns we have not dealt with yet. One is called *strong-stress meter*. Here the rhythm of the line is dependent on four strong metric stresses with no set number of metric weak stresses between them. There's usually a pause or split in the middle of such lines. The lines are usually end-stopped (that is, the sense does not run unbrokenly over the line end, as it does in line 3 of passage 8 above). The stresses are usually underscored by a repetition of sounds (usually consonant sounds), as in the following:

> This is a wild land, country of my choice,
>> With harsh craggy mountain, moor ample and bare.
> Seldom in these acres is heard any voice
>> But voice of cold water that runs here and there
>> Through rocks and lank heather growing without care.   5
> No mice in the heath run nor no birds cry
> For fear of the dark speck that floats in the sky.

> —From *Rocky Acres*
> ROBERT GRAVES (1895–   )

The difference between these lines and more normally metrical lines can be seen if the stanza is written metrically (which at once destroys much of its effectiveness):

> This land is very wild, this land that is my choice,
>> With harsh and craggy mountains, vast and cold and bare.
> Seldom in these acres is heard any voice
>> But voice of icy water running here and there
>> Through rocks and heather lank and past the foxes' lair.   5
> No mice will run in the heath and birds will never cry
> For fear of all the dark specks that float up in the sky.

Since in strong-stress meter the number of unstressed syllables is relatively unimportant, it doesn't make much sense to talk about its metrical feet, even though many lines can be analyzed in terms of the kinds of meters we've been discussing. The important thing is to give all the stresses their due—to emphasize the stress pattern created. Read the following four lines and try to decide where the strong stresses fall:

> The world is charged with the grandeur of God.
>> It will flame out, like shining from shook foil;
>> It gathers to a greatness, like the ooze of oil
> Crushed. Why do men then now not reck his rod?

> —From *God's Grandeur*
>> GERARD MANLEY HOPKINS (1844–1889)

The dominance of the strong stresses in this kind of meter can be seen if we rewrite the lines, adding eight extra syllables:

> The heavens are gloried with the grandeur of God.
>> It will flame outward, like the shining from shaken foil;
>> It will gather to a greatness, like the oozing of oil
> Crushed. Why do men then now not reckon with his rod?

We don't say that the additions leave the rhythm of Hopkins's poem unmarred, but simply that the strong-stress pattern is so powerful rhythmically that the added syllables can't altogether destroy it or submerge it. If eight syllables were thus added to four lines of iambic meter, there would be no rhythm left.

Before discussing what is called "free verse," a third major kind of rhythmic structure, let's look at a few more examples of strong-stress meter. The first two are so regular that they can as well be considered

conventionally metered. In like manner, Auden's "O Where Are You Going?" (p. 116) can be considered strong-stressed as well as anapestic.

> Where the gray seas glitter and the sharp tides shift,
> And the sea-folk labor and the red sails lift.
>
> > —From *Lepanto*
> > GILBERT KEITH CHESTERTON (1874–1936)

> Till the slow sea rise and the sheer cliff crumble,
>   Till terrace and meadow the deep gulfs drink,
> Till the strength of the waves of the high tides humble
>   The fields that lessen, the rocks that shrink, . . .
>
> > —From *A Forsaken Garden*
> > ALGERNON CHARLES SWINBURNE (1837–1909)

In many modern poems the rhythmic structure is a mixture of con-
ventional meters and strong-stress meter. See how well you can distinguish the ingredients of this mixture in the following examples:

> Phlebas the Phoenician, a fortnight dead,
> Forgot the cry of gulls, and the deep sea swell
> And the profit and loss.
>   A current under sea
> Picked his bones in whispers. As he rose and fell   5
> He passed the stages of his age ar ⁻ ·outh
> Entering the whirlpool.
>   Gentile or Jew
> O you who turn the wheel and look to windward,
> Consider Phlebas, who was once handsome and tall as you.   10
>
> > —From *The Waste Land, IV*
> > T. S. ELIOT (1888–1965)

> There head falls forward, fatigued at evening,
> And dreams of home,
> Waving from window, spread of welcome,
> Kissing of wife under single sheet;
> But waking sees   5
> Bird-flocks nameless to him, through doorway voices
> Of new men making another love.
>
> > —From *Something Is Bound to Happen*
> > W. H. AUDEN (1907–1973)

Deep with the first dead lies London's daughter,
Robed in the long friends,
The grains beyond age, the dark veins of her mother
Secret by the unmourning water
Of the riding Thames.   5
After the first death, there is no other.

> —From *A Refusal to Mourn the Death,*
> *by Fire, of a Child in London*
> DYLAN THOMAS (1914–1953)

vi

"Free verse" is not verse in the sense in which we've been using the term so far. It would be better to call it a poetic rhythm free *from* verse —free from any kind of definite metrical pattern, although any free verse poem has occasional lines and phrases with obvious metrical regularity.

Yet there is pattern in free verse, and it's achieved in a number of ways: through the repetition of sounds, words, and grammatical structures; through the paralleling of ideas; even through the use of special printing effects on the page, as in "plato told him" (p. 28). Some very subtle rhythms have been achieved in free verse poems, as should be clear from the following examples.

[11]   *Twenty-third Psalm*

KING JAMES VERSION

The Lord is my shepherd; I shall not want.
He maketh me to lie down in green pastures;
He leadeth me beside the still waters;
He restoreth my soul;
He leadeth me in the paths of righteousness for His name's sake.   5
Yea, though I walk through the valley of the shadow of death,
I will fear no evil: for Thou art with me;
Thy rod and Thy staff they comfort me.
Thou preparest a table before me in the presence of mine enemies:
Thou anointest my head with oil; my cup runneth over.   10
Surely goodness and mercy shall follow me all the days of my life.
And I shall dwell in the house of the Lord forever.

[12]   *When I Heard the Learn'd Astronomer*
WALT WHITMAN (1819–1892)

When I heard the learn'd astronomer,
When the proofs, the figures, were ranged in columns before me,
When I was shown the charts and diagrams, to add, divide, and
    measure them,
When I sitting heard the astronomer where he lectured with much
    applause in the lecture room,
How soon unaccountable I became tired and sick,   5
Till rising and gliding out I wander'd off by myself,
In the mystical moist night-air, and from time to time,
Look'd up in perfect silence at the stars.

[13]   From *Snake*
D. H. LAWRENCE (1885–1930)

He lifted his head from his drinking, as cattle do,
And looked at me vaguely, as drinking cattle do,
And flickered his two-forked tongue from his lips, and mused a
    moment,
And stooped and drank a little more,
Being earth brown, earth golden from the burning burning bowels
    of the earth   5
On the day of Sicilian July, with Etna smoking.

QUESTIONS

1 ★ In poems 11 and 12 what kinds of repetition give a sense of pattern?

2 ★ In poem 12 how does the line length in the first four lines and the
    repetition of the "when" clauses support the meaning of those lines?
    Does the growing length underscore the speaker's growing irritation?

3 ★ In passage 13 how has Lawrence handled the verbs in the first four
    lines to help give a pattern to the poem? What other devices of repeti-
    tion has he used? What purpose is served by the repetition and promi-
    nent placement of "and"?

SOUND

i

Sound, like rhythm, is a factor in everyday speech that the poet puts to maximum use. Sound, as a matter of fact, exerts a rather decisive influence upon rhythm in poetry, as you may have noticed when studying the questions in the preceding two sections. Frost, for instance, in his poem about the old dog (p. 87), makes us pronounce "old dog barks backward" with four heavy stresses, partly because the grammatical arrangement (the syntax) calls for four such speech stresses, as we've seen, and partly because the words begin and end with consonants that compel us to rearrange our lips and tongue as we move from one word to the next; the words can't be hurried up or run together. Coleridge obtains the reverse effect with his illustration of the anapest—"With a leap and a bound the swift anapests throng." To see how far sound and syntax, operating together, control rhythm, try to give the same anapestic swing that you gave to Coleridge's line to this one, which has exactly the same number of syllables:

Rooms filled fast, watched pots fumed, cars parked wide, all hell heaved.

Like rhythm, sound is used in poetry to give pleasure for its own sake and to enhance or clarify meaning. Repetition of sound is often inherently enjoyable (although an excess of it may be highly annoying). The pleasure of repeating sounds is one reason (there are others, to be sure) for the appeal of limericks, where sounds repeat each other thick and fast:

> There once was a man from Nantucket
> Who kept all his cash in a bucket;
>   But his daughter, named Nan,
>   Ran away with a man,
> And as for the bucket, Nantucket.   5
>
> But he followed the pair to Pawtucket—
> The man and the girl with the bucket;
>   And he said to the man
>   He was welcome to Nan,
> But as for the bucket, Pawtucket.   10
>
>   ANONYMOUS

The pleasure of repeating sounds also has something to do with the enduring vogue of comic jingles:

It isn't the cough
That carries you off;
It's the coffin
They carry you off in.

ANONYMOUS

Pleasure in repetition also helps account for the persistence of all kinds of rhymes for counting out ("Eenie, meenie, meinie, mo"); for jogging the memory ("Thirty days hath September"); for circulating oddments of practical wisdom ("Early to bed, early to rise"); and for posing riddles:

Little Nancy Etticoat
With a white petticoat
And a red nose;
She has no feet or hands,
The longer she stands   5
The shorter she grows.

ANONYMOUS

Notice how the repetition in "Women" brightens the corner where we happen to be:

I like lemon on my salmon,
Some like salmon plain.
It is much the same with women,
By and large and in the main.

If you want a chain reaction,   5
Leave your chain out in the rain.
It is much the same with women,
By and large and in the main.

Once when I was just a human,
Someone tampered with my brain.   10
It is much the same with women,
By and large and in the main.

—*Women*
ANONYMOUS

But we notice again in these samples what we noticed before with rhythm—that simple repetition is not enough. To create pleasure rather than distaste there must be change as well. The dominant form of recurrence-with-change in the sound of poetry is *rhyme*, as in "brain" and "main" above, or "off" and "cough."

ii

Other forms of recurrence-with-change, all closely related to rhyme, are (1) *assonance,* a term which usually refers to the recurrence of vowel sounds in the presence of changing consonant sounds, as in "chain" and "same" in "Women"; (2) *consonance,* which usually refers to the recurrence of consonant sounds, especially final consonant sounds in the presence of differing vowel sounds, as in "bitch" and "botched" in "There Died a Myriad" (p. 36); and (3) *alliteration,* which refers to recurrence of initial sounds, especially initial consonant sounds, as in "like" and "lemon" or "some" and "salmon" above. These names are of no particular importance, but the effects they stand for *are* important, and will be found in all poetry in obvious or subtle ways.

Consider the following excerpt from a poem that makes much of sound effects.

[1]   From *Lepanto*

GILBERT KEITH CHESTERTON (1874–1936)

Strong gongs groaning as the guns boom far,
  Don John of Austria is going to the war;
Stiff flags straining in the night-blasts cold,
In the gloom black-purple, in the glint old-gold,
Torchlight crimson on the copper kettledrums,   5
Then the tuckets,° then the trumpets, then the cannon, and he
      comes.
Don John laughing in the brave beard curled,
Spurning of his stirrups like the thrones of all the world,
Holding his head up for a flag of all the free.
Lovelight of Spain—hurrah!   10
Death-light of Africa!
Don John of Austria
Is riding to the sea.

°**tuckets:** fanfares.

CONSIDERATIONS

1 This is a passage from a poem on the battle of Lepanto, where, in the sixteenth century, the Moslems were thrown back from the gates of Christian Europe. The lines contain several instances of (a) assonance, (b) consonance, and (c) alliteration. Point them out. Where is rhyme found, apart from the ends of lines?

2 Indicate seven instances in the first five lines where the sound and syntax have forced a succession of three heavy stresses. Why is this pattern so often repeated? What relation does it have to what the passage is saying? What causes a change in the movement in line 6 and how does that change support what is said? How is the last word of line 11 given an unusual pronunciation? Is this appropriate?

3 In some poetry, sound is allowed to become so powerful that it distracts our attention from the sense—hypnotizes us, so to speak, and then passes off shoddy goods on us. Do you detect any signs of this problem in the foregoing passage? In line 4, for instance, could "gloom" and "glint" change places without loss in sense? With improvement in sense? Does "crimson" in line 5 seem to have been chosen for its sense?

Here's another excerpt, also from a poem much concerned with sound:

[2] From *General William Booth Enters into Heaven*

VACHEL LINDSAY (1879–1931)

> Booth led boldly with his big bass drum—
> (Are you washed in the blood of the Lamb?)
> The Saints smiled gravely and they said: "He's come."
> (Are you washed in the blood of the Lamb?)
> Walking lepers followed, rank on rank,   5
> Lurching bravos from the ditches dank,
> Drabs from the alleyways and drug fiends pale—
> Minds still passion-ridden, soul-powers frail:—
> Vermin-eaten saints with moldly breath,
> Unwashed legions with the ways of Death—   10
> (Are you washed in the blood of the Lamb?)

CONSIDERATIONS

General William Booth, founder and longtime head of the Salvation Army, devoted his life to the service of the outcasts of society. The refrain "Are you washed in the blood of the Lamb?" is a familiar revivalist's cry, meaning roughly: Are you cleansed of sin by your belief in Christ?

1   What is the metrical pattern of the stanza? The rhyme pattern?

2   How has Lindsay used sound and syntax to accentuate the picture of General William Booth (pounding his "big bass drum") leading the triumphant parade of the "down and out" into Heaven?

3   What would be lost if the refrain "Are you washed in the blood of the Lamb?" were eliminated?

Comment on the part played by assonance, consonance, alliteration, and rhyme in the following. What is the metrical pattern of each?

> When the hounds of spring are on winter's traces,
>   The mother of months in meadow or plain
> Fills the shadows and windy places
>   With lisp of leaves and ripple of rain;
>
>   —From the "Chorus" of *Atalanta in Calydon*
>   ALGERNON CHARLES SWINBURNE (1837–1909)

> Till the slow sea rise and the sheer cliff crumble,
>   Till terrace and meadow the deep gulfs drink,
> Till the strength of the waves of the high tides humble
>   The fields that lessen, the rocks that shrink,
> Here now in his triumph where all things falter,   5
>   Stretched out on the spoils that his own hand spread,
> As a god self-slain on his own strange altar,
>   Death lies dead.
>
>   —From *A Forsaken Garden*
>   ALGERNON CHARLES SWINBURNE (1837–1909)

> In Xanadu did Kubla Khan
>   A stately pleasure-dome decree:
> Where Alph, the sacred river, ran
>   Through caverns measureless to man
> Down to a sunless sea.   5

So twice five miles of fertile ground
With walls and towers were girdled round:

—From *Kubla Khan*
SAMUEL TAYLOR COLERIDGE (1772–1834)

In the following poem, sound is used with great subtlety. Examine it
carefully:

[3]   *O Where Are You Going?*
W. H. AUDEN (1907–1973)

"O where are you going?" said reader to rider,
"That valley is fatal when furnaces burn,
Yonder's the midden° whose odors will madden,
That gap is the grave where the tall return."

"O do you imagine," said fearer to farer,   5
"That dusk will delay on your path to the pass,
Your diligent looking discover the lacking
Your footsteps feel from granite to grass?"

"O what was that bird," said horror to hearer,
"Did you see that shape in the twisted trees?   10
Behind you swiftly the figure comes softly,
The spot on your skin is a shocking disease?"

"Out of this house"—said rider to reader,
"Yours never will"—said farer to fearer,
"They're looking for you"—said hearer to horror,   15
As he left them there, as he left them there.

CONSIDERATIONS

1 The poem abounds in assonance, consonance, and alliteration. Indicate several instances of each.

°**midden:** dunghill.

2   What impulses of human behavior are referred to in the terms "reader," "fearer," and "horror"? What impulses are referred to in "rider," "farer," and "hearer"?

3   If we think of "reader" and "rider," "fearer" and "farer," and "horror" and "hearer" as standing for opposite impulses, what is the advantage of the fact that the pairs sound *somewhat alike?*

4   What questions are asked in each of the first three stanzas and what warnings (in a sense, answers) are given by the questioner? Notice, for instance, that lines 11 and 12 are in statement form but with a question intonation pattern (determined by the question mark). What answers are given in stanza four?

5   In how many respects does stanza four differ from the rest? What reason might the poet have for making it different? Why isn't the last line of the poem:

> As they left them there, as they left them there.

or

> As he left him there, as he left him there.

iii

Apart from giving pleasure, sound in poetry—like rhythm—may contribute powerfully to meaning, as we've already suggested in some of the questions to preceding poems. In some cases, and to a limited extent, the poet achieves this contribution to meaning by actual imitation. That is to say, a few words—called *onomatopoeic* words—have sounds that more or less imitate their meanings; examples are "snap," "crackle," and "buzz." Even when word sound doesn't imitate meaning, however, skillful placement of a word may be used to reinforce meaning or some aspect of it. In the lines by Tennyson quoted in an earlier section (p. 89), two words with sounds that partly imitate their meanings, "clanged" and "rang," are so placed among other sounds that all of them together tend to support the idea of armor echoing on rock ("clanged," "crag," "rang," "sharp-smitten," "dint"):

> . . . and all to left and right
> The bare black cliff clanged round him, as he based
> His foot on juts of slippery crag that rang
> Sharp-smitten with the dint of armèd heels.

The following stanza uses no words at all whose sounds imitate their meaning, yet rhythm and sound together are made to support the idea of a rooster's crowing:

> Then one he singles from the crew,
> And cheers the happy hen;
> With "How do you do," and "How do you do,"
> And "How do you do" again.

> —From *The Beggar's Opera*, II, iv
> JOHN GAY (1685–1732)

In English poetry there's almost no limit to the possible range of such effects. Here's John Milton supporting with an array of gutturals (hard sounds like *g* and *k*), labials (explosive sounds made with the lips, often used to express strong feelings of anger or revulsion), and nasals (sounds partly made in the nose, like *m* and *n*) the idea of primitive ferocity in a certain pagan god, *Moloch*. (The *Ammonites* were an Old Testament people. *Rabba* was their capital. *Argob* and *Basan* were districts in their territory, which lay between the rivers *Jabbok* and *Arnon*, east of the Jordan.)

> First, *Moloch*, horrid king, besmeared with blood
> Of human sacrifice, and parents' tears;
> Though, for the noise of drums and timbrels loud,
> Their children's cries unheard° that passed through fire
> To his grim idol. Him the Ammonite   5
> Worshiped in Rabba and her watery plain,
> In Argob and in Basan, to the stream
> Of utmost Arnon.

> —From *Paradise Lost*, I
> JOHN MILTON (1608–1674)

Here's Alexander Pope supporting with round, empty, echoing *nd* and *um* sounds his description of a contemporary's poetry as mostly noise. Notice also the use of *internal rhyme* to help emphasize the sound pattern.

°**unheard**: were unheard.

Rend with tremendous sound your ears asunder,
With gun, drum, trumpet, blunderbuss, and thunder.

> —From *The First Satire of the Second Book
> of Horace Imitated*
> ALEXANDER POPE (1688–1744)

Here's Robert Browning supporting with quick explosive sounds the idea of a match being scratched:

A tap at the pane, the quick sharp scratch
And blue spurt of a lighted match,

> —From *Meeting at Night*
> ROBERT BROWNING (1812–1889)

and, with very different sounds, the idea of a small boat beaching in wet sand:

As I gain the cove with pushing prow,
And quench its speed i' the slushy sand.

> —*Ibid.*

But the contribution of sound to meaning is by no means always so clear-cut as in these illustrations. Often all that we can say truthfully is that the sound in some obscure but important way does or does not harmonize with meaning. Consider this stanza, for example, which is sung as a dirge over a young girl believed to be dead:

Fear no more the heat o' the sun,
  Nor the furious winter's rages:
Thou thy worldly task hast done,
  Home art gone, and ta'en thy wages:
Golden lads and girls all must,   5
As chimney sweepers, come to dust.

> —From *Cymbeline*, IV, ii
> WILLIAM SHAKESPEARE (1564–1616)

Every experienced reader of poetry would agree that sound and sense in this poem are strikingly attuned to each other, but it's doubtful whether any one of them would describe the attunement in the same way, for it resists being put into words. Perhaps the very most we can suggest in such a case is that the sound is quiet, sweetly flowing, unobtrusive, and thus chimes with the poem's statement that death is a repose, and even possibly a fulfillment, to which all of us will come.

In the following poem, "Velvet Shoes," try to indicate as specifically as possible how sound seems to match sense. Perhaps we should say that sound *makes* sense in this poem. Literally, snow is cold and wet and not very much like "velvet." Is the snow cold or wet here? Is there any need for protection against it?

> Let us walk in the white snow
>   In a soundless space;
> With footsteps quiet and slow,
>   At a tranquil pace,
>   Under veils of white lace.   5
>
> I shall go shod in silk
>   And you in wool,
> White as white cow's milk,
>   More beautiful
>   Than the breast of a gull.   10
>
> We shall walk through the still town
>   In a windless peace;
> We shall step upon white down,
>   Upon silver fleece,
>   Upon softer than these.   15
>
> We shall walk in velvet shoes:
>   Wherever we go
> Silence will fall like dews
>   On white silence below.
>   We shall walk in the snow.   20

> —*Velvet Shoes*
> ELINOR WYLIE (1885–1928)

In a wholly different way sound also matches sense in the following poem. Each stanza says essentially the same thing. The title, "In Tenebris" means "In Darkness," the darkness of spiritual numbness and deadness, summed up in the last word of the poem, "unhope." How does the shortness of the lines, the distorted syntax (making the reading difficult), and the word choice underscore the deadness the speaker feels?

[4]   *In Tenebris (I)*
                     THOMAS HARDY (1840–1928)

> Wintertime nighs;
> But my bereavement pain
> It cannot bring again:
>   Twice no one dies.
>
> Flower-petals flee;   5
> But since it once hath been,
> No more that severing scene
>   Can harrow me.
>
> Birds faint in dread:
> I shall not lose old strength   10
> In the lone frost's black length:
>   Strength long since fled!
>
> Leaves freeze to dun;
> But friends cannot turn cold
> This season as of old   15
>   For him with none.
>
> Tempests may scath;
> But love cannot make smart
> Again this year his heart
>   Who no heart hath.   20
>
> Black is night's cope;
> But death will not appall
> One who, past doubtings all,
>   Waits in unhope.

CONSIDERATIONS

1 The normal syntax of lines 2–3 would be "But it [wintertime] cannot bring again the pain of my bereavement." What is the normal syntax of lines 6–8 and 18–20? What is the effect of the distortions?

2 What double meanings are there in "cope" (line 21) and "appall" (line 22)? What difference would there be if the last line were the more normal:

> Waits with no hope.

IV
DEVICES
OF COMPRESSION:
The Poet's Shorthand

OVERSTATEMENT

i

Since poetry is, among other things, a way of saying much in little, devices of compression and concentration, devices that help pack maximum meaning into minimum space, are essential to it.

Overstatement is one way of obtaining maximum emphasis, with economy. In overstatement, we emphasize what we mean by saying more than we literally mean, or at least more than is literally true. On this account, overstatement occurs with particular frequency and abandon in love poems, of all periods and at all levels of sophistication.

> You're the Nile,
>   You're the Tower of Pisa,
> You're the smile
>   Of the Mona Lisa . . .
> I'm a worthless check,   5
>   A total wreck,
>   A flop,
> But if, baby, I'm the bottom, you're the top!

> —From *You're the Top*
> COLE PORTER (1895–1964)

A violet by a mossy stone
    Half hidden from the eye!
—Fair as a star, when only one
    Is shining in the sky.

—From *She Dwelt Among the Untrodden Ways*
WILLIAM WORDSWORTH (1770–1850)

Till a' the seas gang dry, my dear,
    And the rocks melt wi' the sun;
And I will luve thee still, my dear,
    While the sands o' life shall run.

—From *My Luve Is Like a Red, Red Rose*
ROBERT BURNS (1759–1796)

Alas, alas, who's injured by my love?
    What merchant's ships have my sighs drowned?
Who says my tears have overflowed his ground?

—From *The Canonization*
JOHN DONNE (1572–1631)

O, she doth teach the torches to burn bright!
It seems she hangs upon the cheek of night
Like a rich jewel in an Ethiop's ear.

—From *Romeo and Juliet*, I, v
WILLIAM SHAKESPEARE (1564–1616)

We must not suppose, however, that overstatement is used only by lovers or always for purposes of praise. It can serve any type of strong emotion. Here's a satiric instance from a famous political poem of eighteenth-century England:

The midwife laid her hand on his thick skull
With this prophetic blessing, "Be thou dull!"—

—From *Absalom and Achitophel*, II
JOHN DRYDEN (1631–1700)

Here's a tragic instance that we've seen before:

Out, out, brief candle!
Life's but a walking shadow, a poor player

That struts and frets his hour upon the stage
And then is heard no more:

—From *Macbeth*, V, v
WILLIAM SHAKESPEARE (1564–1616)

And here's a comic instance:

O, she misused me past the endurance of a block. An oak but with
one green leaf on it would have answered her. . . . She speaks poniards,°
and every word stabs. If her breath were as terrible as her terminations,°
she would infect to the North star.

—From *Much Ado About Nothing*, II, i
WILLIAM SHAKESPEARE (1564–1616)

ii

Here are three poems illustrating some of the characteristic forms that
overstatement takes.

[1]   *In Order To*

KENNETH PATCHEN (1911–1972)

Apply for the position (I've forgotten now for what) I had to
marry the Second Mayor's daughter by twelve noon. The order arrived
three minutes of.

I already had a wife; the Second Mayor was childless: but I did it.

Next they told me to shave off my father's beard. All right. No
matter that he'd been a eunuch, and had succumbed in early childhood:
I did it, I shaved him.

Then they told me to burn a village; next, a fair-sized town; then,
a city; a bigger city; a small, down-at-heels country; then one of "the
great powers"; then another (another, another)—In fact, they went
right on until they'd told me to burn up every man-made thing on the
face of the earth! And I did it, I burned away every last trace, I left
nothing, nothing of any kind whatever.

°**poniards:** daggers.   °**terminations:** her manner of speaking.

Then they told me to blow it all to hell and gone! And I blew it all to hell and gone (oh, didn't I!) . . .

Now, they said, put it back together again; put it all back the way it was when you started.

Well . . . it was my turn then to tell *them* something. Shucks, I didn't want any job that bad.

[2]   *Constancy*

SIR JOHN SUCKLING (1609–1642)

Out upon it! I have loved
　　Three whole days together;
And am like to love three more,
　　If it prove fair weather.

Time shall molt away his wings,   5
　　Ere he shall discover
In the whole wide world again
　　Such a constant lover.

But the spite on 't is, no praise
　　Is due at all to me;   10
Love with me had made no stays,
　　Had it any been but she.

Had it any been but she,
　　And that very face,
There had been at least ere this   15
　　A dozen dozen in her place.

[3]   *Sonnet 130*

WILLIAM SHAKESPEARE (1564–1616)

My mistress' eyes are nothing like the sun;
Coral is far more red than her lips' red;

If snow be white, why then her breasts are dun;
If hairs be wires, black wires grow on her head.
I have seen roses damasked,° red and white,   5
But no such roses see I in her cheeks,
And in some perfumes is there more delight
Than in the breath that from my mistress reeks.
I love to hear her speak, yet well I know
That music hath a far more pleasing sound.   10
I grant I never saw a goddess go;
My mistress, when she walks, treads on the ground:
    And yet, by heaven, I think my love as rare
    As any she belied with false compare.

CONSIDERATIONS

1 What examples of overstatement do you find in each of the poems?

2 Two of these poems get part of their effect by reversing or parodying a "normal" situation. State for poems 2 and 3 what the "normal" situation would be, and in what respects the poet has reversed or parodied it.

3 According to one critic, poem 1 is about a fact of the human mind. "It is about the mind's ability to become so involved with *means* that it loses sight of *purpose;* so concerned with *processes* that it neglects *values.* If we want to understand how a whole nation could do or acquiesce in doing what the Germans did to the Jews under Hitler, this is the appalling fact about the mind from which we must begin." Assuming that this analysis of the poem is correct, with what "means" and "processes" does the speaker of the poem become involved? In what sense can he be said to have lost sight of purpose? Of value? Does he become conscious of these again in the end—or is he at the end blinder than ever? The story in the poem reminds us of folk tales and fairy tales—forms of literature associated with children and the childhood of a people. How does this fact help explain the poet's choice of this kind of story to carry his theme?

4 In poem 2, lines 3–4 contain what looks like an implied slur by the lover on his lady. What is the slur? Stanza two contains a handsome

---

°**damasked:** pink.

compliment by the lover to himself. What is it? Stanza three turns the compliment to himself into a compliment to the lady. How? In stanza four the implied slur on the lady of stanza one is turned into a further high compliment to her. How?

5 How is the apparent slur turned into a compliment in poem 3?

iii

Now consider these other poems that employ overstatement.

[4]   *Sonnet 18*

WILLIAM SHAKESPEARE (1564–1616)

Shall I compare thee to a summer's day?
Thou art more lovely and more temperate.
Rough winds do shake the darling buds of May,
And summer's lease hath all too short a date.
Sometime too hot the eye of heaven shines,   5
And often is his gold complexion dimmed.
And every fair from fair sometime declines,
By chance or nature's changing course untrimmed.°
But thy eternal summer shall not fade,
Nor lose possession of that fair thou owest,°   10
Nor shall Death brag thou wander'st in his shade
When in eternal lines to time thou grow'st.
   So long as men can breathe, or eyes can see,
   So long lives this, and this gives life to thee.

CONSIDERATIONS

1 What does the first line mean? In other words, is it a question or a statement in the form of a question?

2 In what ways is the person addressed compared with and made superior to "a summer's day"? What shift in the comparison serves

---

°**untrimmed:** deprived of ornamentation.   °**owest:** own.

to make the exaggeration acceptable and not just fancifully complimentary? In what sense will the lady's superiority never diminish? Why is "lines" in line 12 the key word of the comparison? (What is the "this" of line 14?)

3   Put the last two lines into your own words.

4   Which of the two sonnets, Sonnet 130 or Sonnet 18, seems most complimentary and why? How do they differ as examples of overstatement used to tell a truth?

[5]   *I Taste a Liquor Never Brewed*
            EMILY DICKINSON (1830–1886)

I taste a liquor never brewed,
From tankards scooped in pearl;
Not all the vats upon the Rhine
Yield such an alcohol!

Inebriate of air am I,   5
And debauchee of dew,
Reeling, through endless summer days,
From inns of molten blue.

When landlords turn the drunken bee
Out of the foxglove's door,   10
When butterflies renounce their drams,
I shall but drink the more!

Till seraphs swing their snowy hats,
And saints to windows run,
To see the little tippler   15
Leaning against the sun!

CONSIDERATIONS

1   What is the "liquor never brewed" that the speaker tastes? What does "pearl" stand for in line 2? Explain as fully as possible each reference that develops the drinking metaphor.

2   What specifically is the exaggeration of stanza three? Could the events
    suggested in lines 9–11 comes to pass? If they couldn't, what does the
    speaker gain by saying that *when* they do, "I shall but drink the more"?

3   How would you reply to someone who argued that the comparison is
    inappropriate?

[6]   *As I Walked Out One Evening*
                       W. H. AUDEN (1907–1973)

As I walked out one evening,
    Walking down Bristol Street,
The crowds upon the pavement
    Were fields of harvest wheat.

And down by the brimming river   5
    I heard a lover sing
Under an arch of the railway:
    "Love has no ending.

I'll love you, dear, I'll love you
    Till China and Africa meet,   10
And the river jumps over the mountain
    And the salmon sing in the street.

I'll love you till the ocean
    Is folded and hung up to dry,
And the seven stars go squawking   15
    Like geese about the sky.

The years shall run like rabbits,
    For in my arms I hold
The Flower of the Ages,
    And the first love of the world."   20

But all the clocks in the city
    Began to whirr and chime:

"O let not Time deceive you,
    You cannot conquer Time.

In the burrows of the Nightmare   25
    Where Justice naked is,
Time watches from the shadow
    And coughs when you would kiss.

In headaches and in worry
    Vaguely life leaks away,   30
And Time will have his fancy
    Tomorrow or today.

Into many a green valley
    Drifts the appalling snow;
Time breaks the threaded dances   35
    And the diver's brilliant bow.

O plunge your hands in water,
    Plunge them in up to the wrist;
Stare, stare in the basin
    And wonder what you've missed.   40

The glacier knocks in the cupboard,
    The desert sighs in the bed,
And the crack in the teacup opens
    A lane to the land of the dead,

Where the beggars raffle the banknotes   45
    And the Giant is enchanting to Jack,
And the Lily-white Boy is a Roarer,
    And Jill goes down on her back.

O look, look in the mirror,
    O look in your distress;   50
Life remains a blessing
    Although you cannot bless.

O stand, stand at the window
   As the tears scald and start;
You shall love your crooked neighbor   55
   With your crooked heart."

It was late, late in the evening,
   The lovers they were gone;
The clocks had ceased their chiming,
   And the deep river ran on.   60

CONSIDERATIONS

1 Who is the main speaker in the poem? What speakers does he over-hear?

2 The mood of the speaker is implied in his instinctive comparison of the crowds he sees to "harvest wheat." What is normally the fate of "harvest wheat"? What is thus suggested about the crowds? How does this comparison fit in with what the clocks seem to say to the speaker?

3 Is the overstatement by the lover in stanzas three through five so ludicrous as to be completely insincere, or is it meant to be flatteringly amusing, or, perhaps, a combination of the two? The answer to the question lies in an assessment of the clocks' reply to the lover. What is the tone of the exaggerated reply—bantering, mocking, serious?

4 What is true about human behavior that validates the statement "You cannot conquer Time"? If the clocks (ironically, Time) use exaggerated statements to answer the lover's exaggeration, what is gained by doing so? The answer is essentially good, sober advice: Why isn't it given soberly? What is the advice? Do the "lovers" hear the advice? Would they pay attention to it if they did? (Consider the implications of the final stanza.)

[7]   *The Scholars*

WILLIAM BUTLER YEATS (1865–1939)

Bald heads forgetful of their sins,
Old, learned, respectable bald heads

Edit and annotate the lines
That young men, tossing on their beds,
Rhymed out in love's despair   5
To flatter beauty's ignorant ear.

All shuffle there; all cough in ink;
All wear the carpet with their shoes;
All think what other people think;
All know the man their neighbor knows.   10
Lord, what would they say
Did their Catullus° walk that way?

CONSIDERATIONS

1 Why is the title of the poem "The Scholars"? Is the overstatement about the "young men" unflattering in the same sense that the overstatement about the "bald heads" is?

2 What were "their sins" (line 1)? What are their sins now? Explain lines 7–10.

3 The speaker thinks that the old men who annotate passionate poets' lines would exclaim if they saw "their Catullus" alive. Why does the speaker think so?

[8]   *Incident*

COUNTEE CULLEN (1903–1946)

Once riding in old Baltimore,
    Heart-filled, head-filled with glee,
I saw a Baltimorean
    Keep looking straight at me.

Now I was eight and very small,   5
    And he was no whit bigger,

°**Catullus:** a Roman poet who celebrated, in terms we would consider bluntly realistic, the life and loves of a young man about town. The realism has often disappeared in "translation."

And so I smiled, but he poked out
His tongue and called me "Nigger."

I saw the whole of Baltimore
From May until December: 10
Of all the things that happened there
That's all that I remember.

CONSIDERATIONS

1 What *is* the "incident" that the poem describes? What are we told
in lines 2, 5–6 that accounts for what the speaker did? What are we
told in lines 1, 3–4, that accounts for what the "Baltimorean" did?
What added effect is obtained here by calling Baltimore "old Baltimore"? by calling an eight-year-old a "Baltimorean"? by saying that
he "poked" out his tongue rather than (saying) "stuck" it out?

2 Does the last stanza contain an overstatement? If so, what literal truth
is it used to convey? If not, explain how it can be a literal truth as it
stands.

3 What do the formal characteristics of the poem—its regularities of
rhyme and rhythm, its division into equal stanzas, its quiet language—
contribute to its total effect? (Note that the speaker does not apply
any shrill language to the other boy or to the event, even in retro-
spect: the boy remains a "Baltimorean" and the event simply an
"Incident.")

UNDERSTATEMENT

Understatement is of course precisely the opposite of overstatement. In
understatement we emphasize what we mean by saying less than we
literally mean, or less than is literally true. For an effective example, we
may look back for a moment at Robert Frost's "Out, Out—" (p. 69). The
speech in *Macbeth* (p. 70) to which, as we saw, Frost's title alludes takes
the expression of futility and despair about as far as overstatement will
go. Macbeth speaks as if the analogy, which does indeed exist, between
a human life and an actor's "hour" upon the stage were the literal truth

about the lives of men and women. Frost's speaker in "Out, Out—" moves in the reverse direction. He also communicates a sense of futility and despair, but by understatement. In his description of the boy's death, no word that does justice to the literal situation is allowed to appear. No one—so far as we are told—gasps, swallows hard, swears, prays, or is even slightly shaken. Instead,

> Little—less—nothing! and that ended it.
> No more to build on there. And they, since they
> Were not the one dead, turned to their affairs.

Hardy obtains a somewhat analogous effect, though slighter, with the description of war that he puts in his speaker's mouth in the last stanza of "The Man He Killed" (p. 34): "Yes; quaint and curious war is! . . ." This again is a good deal less than the situation justifies, since it comes from a man who, obviously of a sympathetic and kindly nature, has been forced by war to kill a fellow human being. But what Hardy's speaker leaves out we tend to fill in with our own imaginations, and this is one reason for the great effectiveness of understatement in obtaining emphasis. Consider whether or not understatement is effective in the following two examples:

[1]   *Portrait*

E. E. CUMMINGS (1894–1962)

Buffalo Bill's
defunct
     who used to
     ride a watersmooth-silver
               stallion   5
and   break   onetwothreefourfive   pigeonsjustlikethat
                             Jesus

he was a handsome man
             and what i want to know is
how do you like your blueeyed boy   10
Mister Death

[2]   *Losses*

RANDALL JARRELL (1914–1965)

It was not dying: everybody died.
It was not dying: we had died before
In the routine crashes—and our fields°
Called up the papers, wrote home to our folks,
And the rates° rose, all because of us.   5
We died on the wrong page of the almanac,
Scattered on mountains fifty miles away;
Diving on haystacks, fighting with a friend,
We blazed up on the lines° we never saw.
We died like ants or pets or foreigners.   10
(When we left high school nothing else had died
For us to figure we had died like.)

In our new planes, with our new crews, we bombed
The ranges by the desert or the shore,
Fired at towed targets, waited for our scores—   15
And turned into replacements and woke up
One morning, over England, operational.
It wasn't different: but if we died
It was not an accident but a mistake
(But an easy one for anyone to make).   20
We read our mail and counted up our missions—
In bombers named for girls, we burned
The cities we had learned about in school—
Till our lives wore out; our bodies lay among
The people we had killed and never seen.   25
When we lasted long enough they gave us medals;
When we died they said, "Our casualties were low."
They said, "Here are the maps"; we burned the cities.

It was not dying—no, not ever dying;

°**fields:** airfields   °**rates:** insurance rates   °**lines:** powerlines.

But the night I died I dreamed that I was dead, 30
And the cities said to me: "Why are you dying?
We are satisfied, if you are; but why did I die?"

CONSIDERATIONS

1 What examples of understatement are there in any of the poems used to illustrate overstatement? Consider particularly poems 1, 2, and 3.

2 "Portrait" treats a serious subject—the death of a well-known figure—in a lighthearted manner. The "i" of the poem is no boy, but he uses the idiom of boyish wonder to suggest that even though Buffalo Bill is dead, he remains just as vital as ever: he's a "blueeyed boy" who has moved in with old "Mister Death," who certainly ought to appreciate what he got. Show how the understatement, the almost irreverent attitude toward death, actually gives the fact of death more proper reverence than a somber treatment would give. Consider the details of the "portrait" of Buffalo Bill in action, the use of such words as "defunct" instead of "dead," and the way the lines are printed on the page.

3 "Losses" is another poem about death. As the title suggests, this poem, too, treats death rather casually: "losses" are things that get added up for use in keeping statistics. What lines clearly establish the pattern of understatement?

4 In "Losses" who is the speaker? What specifically does he recall in the first fifteen lines? In what tone are these experiences recalled? How does line 10 underscore the attitude adopted, and how is it reinforced in lines 11–12? What do lines 16–28 deal with and how have the first twelve lines prepared for the treatment of these experiences?

5 Line 29 repeats the opening words. What deepened meaning have the intervening lines given to them? What is ironic about line 30? How do the last two lines employ both overstatement and understatement?

6 How is understatement used in "My Papa's Waltz" (p. 76)? Consider the use of "romped," "unfrown," "beat time on my head," "waltzed me off to bed," and the almost jingly regularity of the rhythm. How does the speaker communicate the coarse exuberance of the father and the breath-holding fear of the boy? In what sense was the father's drunken dance a "waltz" (to whom?) and in what sense was it not?

IRONY AND PARADOX

i

In overstatement we intensify meaning by saying more than we literally mean or than is literally true. In understatement we intensify meaning by saying less than we literally mean or than is literally true. With *irony* and *paradox* we intensify meaning by saying something different from what we literally mean or from what is literally true. A *paradox* is a compressed way of making a single truth grow from two elements that literally contradict each other: it's a spark that leaps between a negatively and positively charged pole. "Damn with faint praise" (Alexander Pope), "The last shall be first" (New Testament), "The wise through excess of wisdom is made a fool" (Ralph Waldo Emerson), "Poetry is a language that tells us something that cannot be said" (Edwin Arlington Robinson)—all these are paradoxes in that two seemingly contradictory elements generate between them a meaning that cannot be got at so economically in any other way. To explain the idea underlying "Damn with faint praise," for instance, we not only have to use a great many more words than Pope used, but we lose the impact, the shock value, which paradox ordinarily has for us.

Paradox does not absolutely require that its contradictory elements be brought out by contradictory words, as they are in the foregoing examples. We can still detect the contradiction in the idea of a person's being at the end of a line yet somehow getting through a gate sooner than those preceeding him ("The last shall be first"), no matter how it's phrased. Yet there's no doubt that paradox strengthens and moves toward its perfection when the contradictory elements in the situation are underscored by contradictory words; and you'll find it difficult if not impossible in some cases—for example, in the case of the paradox quoted from Emerson —to describe the contradictory situation adequately apart from some form of verbal contradiction.

With *irony* this dependence on wording is not the case. There's a *verbal* irony, very common in our daily speech, which we use when we exclaim "You're a big help!" to someone who has awkwardly knocked all our books out of our hands while he was stooping to pick up our hat; and this kind of irony is found in poetry frequently enough. But the commonest and most powerful form that irony can take, in poetry and literature generally, is that of *situation*, and for this irony no particular wording is required. A man labors all his life, denying himself every pleasure, to lay up a fortune for his children to inherit, and then sees them all die before his own death. A Macbeth murders to get what he thinks he covets only to find it has turned to ashes in his hands. An Oedipus sets out to find the source of the evil that has infected his kingdom and discovers that it is himself. A Proud Maisie walks abroad on a spring morning glowing with thoughts of love and marriage, but actually her bridegroom will be death and her bridal bed the grave. Such ironies as these are ironies of situation.

Related both to irony of situation and to verbal irony is a third form of irony that we usually call *dramatic*. This appears whenever a speaker in a literary work says something with an application or a depth of meaning that we or others see but he doesn't. Thus King Duncan, commenting in *Macbeth* on the treason of one of his most trusted subjects, says, "There's no art to find the mind's construction in the face," just as Macbeth, who is going to prove a traitor very soon, enters the room. Duncan's comment has an application that he doesn't see. Similarly, after the assassination of Julius Caesar in Shakespeare's play of that name, Brutus says to his fellow assassins:

> . . . let us bathe our hands in Caesar's blood
> Up to the elbows, and besmear our swords;
> Then walk we forth, even to the market place,
> And waving our red weapons o'er our heads,
> Let's all cry, "Peace, freedom, and liberty!"   5

—From *Julius Caesar*, III, i
WILLIAM SHAKESPEARE (1564–1616)

In Brutus's speech, there are two layers of dramatic irony. The first lies in the ironical contrast (of which Brutus is wholly unaware) between the bloody assassins and the cry "Peace, freedom, and liberty!" The second lies in the ironical contrast between the "peace, freedom, and liberty" which they wanted to bring Rome and the discord and carnage which, as the rest of the play shows, they actually did bring. The irony of the word "waiting" in the young lady's speech in "Piazza Piece" (p. 40) is also of this dramatic kind when she utters it for the second time: "I am a lady young in beauty, waiting." She's waiting, all right, but she hasn't stopped to think (as we've been made to do) who she's waiting for.

The two poems which follow, "Sir Patrick Spence" and "Ozymandias," are filled with irony of all sorts. The questions on page 142 will help you identify it.

Sir Patrick Spence
                        ANONYMOUS

The king sits in Dumferling toune,°
    Drinking the blude-reid° wine:
"O whar will I get guid° sailor,
    To sail this schip of mine?"

Up and spak an eldern knicht,°   5
    Sat at the kings richt° kne:
"Sir Patrick Spence is the best sailor,
    That sails upon the se."

The king has written a braid° letter,
    And signd it wi his hand,   10
And sent it to Sir Patrick Spence,
    Was walking on the sand.

The first line that Sir Patrick red,
    A loud lauch° lauchèd he;
The next line that Sir Patrick red,   15
    The teir blinded his ee.

"O wha is this has don this deid,
    This ill deid don to me,
To send me out this time o' the yeir,
    To sail upon the se!   20

"Mak hast, mak hast, my mirry men all,
    Our guid schip sails the morne":
"O say na sae,° my master deir,
    For I fear a deadlie storme.

"Late, late yestreen° I saw the new moone,   25
    Wi the auld moone in hir arme,

°**toune:** town.   °**blude-reid:** blood-red.   °**guid:** good.   °**knicht:** knight.
°**richt:** right.   °**braid:** broad (official).   °**lauch:** laugh.   °**na sae:** not so.
°**yestreen:** yesterday evening.

And I feir, I feir, my deir master,
   That we will cum to harme."

O our Scot nobles wer richt laith°
   To weet° their cork-heild schoone;°   30
But lang owre a'° the play wer playd,
   Thair hats they swam aboone.

O lang, lang may their ladies sit,
   Wi thair fans into thair hand,
Or eir they se Sir Patrick Spence   35
   Cum sailing to the land.

O lang, lang may the ladies stand,
   Wi thair gold kems in thair hair,
Waiting for thair ain deir lords,
   For they'll se thame na mair.   40

Haf owre,° haf owre to Aberdour,
   It's fiftie fadom° deip,
And thair lies guid Sir Patrick Spence,
   Wi the Scots lords at his feit.

[2]   *Ozymandias*

PERCY BYSSHE SHELLEY (1792–1822)

I met a traveler from an antique land
Who said: Two vast and trunkless legs of stone
Stand in the desert . . . Near them, on the sand,
Half sunk, a shattered visage lies, whose frown,
And wrinkled lip, and sneer of cold command,   5
Tell that its sculptor well those passions read
Which yet survive, stamped on these lifeless things,
The hand that mocked them, and the heart that fed:

°**laith:** loath (reluctant).   °**weet:** wet.   °**cork-heild schoone:** cork-heeled
shoes.   °**owre a':** before all.   °**owre:** over.   °**fadom:** fathom.

And on the pedestal these words appear:
"My name is Ozymandias, king of kings: 10
Look on my works, ye Mighty, and despair!"
Nothing beside remains. Round the decay
Of that colossal wreck, boundless and bare
The lone and level sands stretch far away.

CONSIDERATIONS

1   In poem 1, what apparently does the King order in his letter (stanza
    three)? Why does Sir Patrick first laugh on reading the order? Why
    later does the tear spring to his eye? What feeling do the Scots nobles
    have about making the trip?

2   Point out two examples of irony of situation in poem 1. There's dra-
    matic irony in the words "guid" and "best" in lines 3 and 7. Explain.
    There's verbal irony in lines 33–36. Explain.

3   In poem 2, whose passions "yet survive . . . the hand that mocked
    them and the heart that fed?" (lines 7–8). Whose "heart" fed them?
    Whose "hand" mocked them? How?

4   What instruction does Ozymandias give to those who pass by the
    pedestal of his statue? Whom did he expect to read these instructions?
    Who actually does read them? Where are the "works" the instructions
    speak of? Whose work actually *has* survived? Is it true that the arts
    of a nation survive most of its other manifestations? What do we have
    left from ancient Egypt? Ancient Greece? Ancient China? What is
    most likely to remain from our age in A.D. 4000, if anything?

5   Poem 2 contains verbal irony, dramatic irony, and irony of situation.
    State where and explain.

ii

Though irony and paradox spring up everywhere in poetry (and in other
forms of literature as well), the following poems contain some particularly
notable examples:

[3]   *The Wood-Pile*

ROBERT FROST (1874–1963)

Out walking in the frozen swamp one gray day,
I paused and said, "I will turn back from here.
No, I will go on farther—and we shall see."
The hard snow held me, save where now and then
One foot went through. The view was all in lines   5
Straight up and down of tall slim trees
Too much alike to mark or name a place by
So as to say for certain I was here
Or somewhere else: I was just far from home.
A small bird flew before me. He was careful   10
To put a tree between us when he lighted,
And say no word to tell me who he was
Who was so foolish as to think what *he* thought.
He thought that I was after him for a feather—
The white one in his tail; like one who takes   15
Everything said as personal to himself.
One flight out sideways would have undeceived him.
And then there was a pile of wood for which
I forgot him and let his little fear
Carry him off the way I might have gone,   20
Without so much as wishing him goodnight.
He went behind it to make his last stand.
It was a cord of maple, cut and split
And piled—and measured, four by four by eight.
And not another like it could I see.   25
No runner tracks in this year's snow looped near it.
And it was older sure than this year's cutting,
Or even last year's or the year's before.
The wood was gray and the bark warping off it
And the pile somewhat sunken. Clematis   30
Had wound strings round and round it like a bundle.
What held it though on one side was a tree

Still growing, and on one a stake and prop,
These latter about to fall. I thought that only
Someone who lived in turning to fresh tasks   35
Could so forget his handiwork on which
He spent himself, the labor of his ax,
And leave it there far from a useful fireplace
To warm the frozen swamp as best it could
With the slow smokeless burning of decay.   40

CONSIDERATIONS

1 Put into your own words the basic irony of the situation involving the
   woodpile. Why was the wood cut in the first place? What will eventually happen to it? How does it make sense to say that it can "warm
   the frozen swamp" with the "smokeless burning of decay"?

2 What other examples of irony are there in the poem? What purpose is
   served by the speaker's encounter with the suspicious bird?

[4]   *To an Athlete Dying Young*
                 A. E. HOUSMAN (1859–1936)

The time you won your town the race
We chaired you through the market place;
Man and boy stood cheering by,
And home we brought you shoulder-high.

Today, the road all runners come,   5
Shoulder-high we bring you home,
And set you at your threshold down,
Townsman of a stiller town.

Smart lad, to slip betimes away
From fields where glory does not stay   10
And early though the laurel grows
It withers quicker than the rose.

Eyes the shady night has shut
Cannot see the record cut,
And silence sounds no worse than cheers   15
After earth has stopped the ears:

Now you will not swell the rout
Of lads that wore their honors out,
Runners whom renown outran
And the name died before the man.   20

So set, before its echoes fade,
The fleet foot on the sill of shade,
And hold to the low lintel up
The still-defended challenge-cup.

And round that early-laureled head   25
Will flock to gaze the strengthless dead,
And find unwithered on its curls
The garland briefer than a girl's.

CONSIDERATIONS

1   What ironic situation is carefully developed in the first two stanzas?
    How has the speaker closely paralleled the two occurrences that would
    seem on the surface to be so removed from each other?

2   How has he prepared for the irony of referring to the dead runner as
    a "smart lad"? What does the "laurel" stand for? The "rose"? Ironically,
    under what conditions can each remain unwithered?

[5]   *Holy Sonnet 10*
                    JOHN DONNE (1572–1631)

Death, be not proud, though some have called thee
Mighty and dreadful, for thou art not so;
For those whom thou think'st thou dost overthrow

Die not, poor Death, nor yet canst thou kill me.
From rest and sleep, which but thy pictures be,   5
Much pleasure, then from thee much more must flow;
And soonest our best men with thee do go,
Rest of their bones and soul's delivery.
Thou'rt slave to fate, chance, kings, and desperate men,
And dost with poison, war, and sickness dwell;   10
And poppy or charms can make us sleep as well,
And better than thy stroke. Why swell'st thou then?
One short sleep past, we wake eternally,
And death shall be no more. Death, thou shalt die.

CONSIDERATIONS

1   What is the paradox stated in the last line of "Holy Sonnet 10"? How
has it been prepared for? In other words, how is the argument developed that leads up to it? (Line 13 asserts the speaker's belief in an
afterlife.) What earlier paradoxes are there?

2   What is the basic metrical pattern? In what lines is it most clearly revealed? What obvious variations are there, and what is their effectiveness in the poem?

3   What is the tone of the poem? Arrogant? Flippant? Smug? Mocking?
Nonchalant? Calm? None of these?

[6]   *What Are Years?*

MARIANNE MOORE (1887–1972)

What is our innocence,
  what is our guilt? All are
    naked, none is safe. And whence
is courage: the unanswered question,
the resolute doubt,—   5
dumbly calling, deafly listening—that
in misfortune, even death,
        encourages others
        and in its defeat, stirs

the soul to be strong? He
sees deep and is glad, who
    accedes to mortality
and in his imprisonment, rises
upon himself as
the sea in a chasm, struggling to be   15
free and unable to be,
    in its surrendering
    finds its continuing.

So he who strongly feels,
behaves. The very bird,   20
    grown taller as he sings, steels
his form straight up. Though he is captive,
his mighty singing
says, satisfaction is a lowly
thing, how pure a thing is joy.   25
    This is mortality,
    this is eternity.

CONSIDERATIONS

1 What questions are raised in the first two lines? What is the answer given in lines 2–3? The question in lines 3–4 is oddly put: "And whence is courage?" Why isn't it the more normal "What is courage?" or "Whence comes courage?" What connection does the question have with the first two questions? Lines 4–10 identify courage in a series of paradoxes. Explain them.

2 Stanzas two and three are built around two extended comparisons. In what terms is courage described in stanza two? What does the sea in a chasm do? What is the paradox in lines 17–18 and how has it been resolved?

3 What is the comparison in stanza three? Where is the bird? Why is "steels" a particularly appropriate verb in the development of the comparison? What is the difference between "satisfaction" and "joy"?

4 What does "this" refer to in lines 26–27? The dictionary meanings of "mortality" ("subject to death") and "eternity" ("not subject to

:em to deny that both words can be applied to the

Paradoxically, how can they be, as demonstrated in

swer to the title?

[7]   *Richard Cory*

EDWIN ARLINGTON ROBINSON (1869–1935)

Whenever Richard Cory went down town,
We people on the pavement looked at him:
He was a gentleman from sole to crown,
Clean favored, and imperially slim.

And he was always quietly arrayed,   5
And he was always human when he talked;
But still he fluttered pulses when he said,
"Good-morning," and he glittered when he walked.

And he was rich—yes, richer than a king—
And admirably schooled in every grace: 10
In fine, we thought that he was everything
To make us wish that we were in his place.

So on we worked, and waited for the light,
And went without the meat, and cursed the bread;
And Richard Cory, one calm summer night,   15
Went home and put a bullet through his head.

QUESTIONS

1 On what does the irony of "Richard Cory" seem to depend? Simply
on the trick ending? Or is it a trick ending? Is the outcome prepared
for in any way? If, in a sense, it isn't prepared for, how does that
fact reinforce the underlying irony of the poem?

2 How carefully has the speaker seen his man? In what terms does he
describe him? Why does he say "from sole to crown" (line 3) instead
of "from head to foot" (ignoring the problem of rhyme for the mo-

ment)? What kind of people think other people "glitter" when they walk, and use phrases like "clean favored" and "quietly arrayed"? What is the speaker trying to suggest about Richard Cory? More important, what does he reveal about his own powers of discrimination? (Remember, he's the same person who uses such language as "went without the meat, and cursed the bread.") How much do people like the speaker understand of those they really don't know? What have these considerations got to do with the problem raised in question 1? What double irony is there in the poem?

[8]   *The Negro*

JAMES A. EMANUEL (1921–   )

> Never saw him.
> Never can.
> Hypothetical,
> Haunting man:
>
> Eyes a-saucer,   5
> Yessir, boss-sir,
> Dice a-clicking,
> Razor flicking.
>
> The-ness froze him
> In a dance.   10
> A-ness never
> Had a chance.

CONSIDERATIONS

1 The point of the poem is obvious: what society has created is a stereotype of "the Negro" that prevents its seeing blacks as individual human beings. In the light of this overall point, explain in detail what the poet means by (a) "Never saw him" (b) "Never can" (c) "Hypothetical" (d) "Haunting" (e) "The-ness froze him." What is the relation of the "hypothetical" man of lines 3–4 to the attributes described in lines 5–8? How do they exemplify "The-ness"? and preclude "A-ness"?

2 Why is the title of the poem appropriate?

[9]   *London*

WILLIAM BLAKE (1757–1827)

I wander through each chartered street,
Near where the chartered Thames does flow,
And mark in every face I meet
Marks of weakness, marks of woe.

In every cry of every man,   5
In every infant's cry of fear,
In every voice, in every ban,
The mind-forged manacles I hear:

How the chimney sweeper's cry
Every blackening church appalls,   10
And the hapless soldier's sigh
Runs in blood down palace walls.

But most, through midnight streets I hear
How the youthful harlot's curse
Blasts the newborn infant's tear,   15
And blights with plagues the marriage hearse.

CONSIDERATIONS

1   Discuss the pattern of ironies that make up Blake's indictment of in-
    human behavior in "London." How can the "manacles" of line 8 be
    "mind-forged"? How and why does the "chimney sweeper's cry"
    appall "every blackening church"? What is "blackening" the church?
    What should the church do about the use of young children as chim-
    ney sweepers? What double meaning is there in "appalls"?

2   In what sense can a soldier's sigh run "in blood down palace walls"?
    What have palaces to do with soldiers? What does "sigh" mean here?

3   Why does the fourth stanza start with "But most"? What is the "youth-
    ful [why "youthful"?] harlot's curse"? How can her curse blast "the
    newborn infant's tear"? How can it blight with "plagues"? Why does
    the speaker conjoin the words "marriage" and "hearse"?

COMPARISON

i

The most important of all devices for saying much in little in poetry is comparison. Our ordinary speech is full of comparisons, and most of us are able to recognize, when we stop to think, those which are conveyed by means of *simile* or *metaphor*. "It seems she hangs upon the cheek of night,/Like a rich jewel in an Ethiop's ear." Romeo says that Juliet is hanging like some adornment on the cheek of night, and then, with the use of "like" to introduce the specific comparison, he likens her to a "jewel" hanging from "an Ethiop's ear." If he had said, "She is a jewel hanging from an Ethiop's ear," we would have what is technically referred to as a *metaphor*. If "like" or "as" is used to make the comparison ("like a rich jewel . . ."), we have a *simile*. Often the word *metaphor* is used in a broader sense to refer to any comparison in which one thing is described in terms of another. In questions on the poems that follow we'll use the term *metaphor* in this broader sense.

We can see the process of metaphor at work in many of the poems we've looked at already. For a few examples: consider: "Like a small gray coffeepot" ("The Gray Squirrel," p. 6); "whereon a dozen staunch and leal/citizens did *graze at*" ("A Man Who Had Fallen Among Thieves," p. 16; notice that here grammar is being used metaphorically, for not only is there the comparison with sheep in "graze," but there's also the grammatical comparison with "gaze at"); "For an old *bitch* gone in the teeth" ("There Died a Myriad," p. 36); "I am a gentleman in a *dust-coat*" ("Piazza Piece," p. 40); "the blond *assassin*" ("Apparently with No Surprise," p. 69); "*Golden* lads and girls all must,/As *chimney sweepers*, come to *dust*" ("Fear No More the Heat o' the Sun," p. 119). You can find other examples in the previous poem, "London," and in the following:

[1]   *Digging for China*

                RICHARD WILBUR (1921–   )

"Far enough down is China," somebody said.
"Dig deep enough and you might see the sky
As clear as at the bottom of a well.
Except it would be real—a different sky.
Then you could burrow down until you came   5
To China! Oh, it's nothing like New Jersey.

There's people, trees, and houses, and all that
But much, much different. Nothing looks the same."

I went and got the trowel out of the shed
And sweated like a coolie all that morning.   10
Digging a hole beside the lilac bush,
Down on my hands and knees. It was a sort
Of praying, I suspect. I watched my hand
Dig deeper and darker, and I tried and tried
To dream a place where nothing was the same.   15
The trowel never did break through to blue.

Before the dream could weary of itself
My eyes were tired of looking into darkness,
My sunbaked head of hanging down a hole.
I stood up in a place I had forgotten,   20
Blinking and staggering while the earth went round
And showed me silver barns, the fields dozing
In palls of brightness, patens growing and gone
In the tides of leaves, and the whole sky china blue.
Until I got my balance back again   25
All that I saw was China, China, China.

CONSIDERATIONS

1 Who is the speaker? What kind of person is he? What kind of person
   is the "somebody" of the first stanza?

2 Explain as fully as possible the metaphors in lines 22–24. Why are the
   barns "silver"? What suggestions are there in "palls of brightness" (be
   sure you know what "palls" are)? What are "patens" and why would
   the speaker in his condition see them "growing and gone/In the tides
   of leaves"? What is ironic and appropriate about "china blue"?

3 What is the speaker looking for? What does he think it will be like?
   Ironically, how does he find it? Is it what he thought (or hoped) it
   would be like? What irony is there in the word "balance" (line 25)?
   What does physical "balance" do to his spiritual equilibrium?

4 How is the poem a metaphor for one kind of human behavior? How do you know that it's spiritual equilibrium the speaker is talking about?

[2] *Harlem*

LANGSTON HUGHES (1902–1967)

What happens to a dream deferred?

Does it dry up
like a raisin in the sun?
Or fester like a sore—
And then run?
Does it stink like rotten meat?   5
Or crust and sugar over—
like a syrupy sweet?

Maybe it just sags
like a heavy load.

Or does it explode?   10

CONSIDERATIONS

1 How would you define the "dream" that Hughes refers to? Why is it "deferred"? Compare and contrast with this dream the one spoken of in Wilbur's poem.

2 The poem tentatively suggests six possible effects that deferment may have on a dream. What does the poet gain from choosing here to be so tentative—from asking rather than telling us?

3 Each of the first five effects is elaborated by a simile that makes the effect claimed seem natural and inevitable—e.g. drying up "like a raisin in the sun," festering "like a sore," and so on. Show how this procedure makes the sixth effect stand out like the very explosion it describes.

ii

With other forms of comparison we may be less familiar than we are
with simile and metaphor, because we have not stopped to realize, as we
used them, what they were. *Allusion* is one of these. Allusion brings objects or ideas together for comparison in precisely the same way that
metaphor and simile do. In the midst of Romeo's combined metaphor and
simile about Juliet, for instance, there's also an allusion—to the Ethiop.
Juliet's youthful beauty lights up the night the way a bright jewel lights
up the cheek of an Ethiopian prince. The reader has to recognize the
allusion to the Ethiopian prince before the comparison can have full
effect. Explanations of allusions that refer to people, to places, to historical
events, or to works of literature can usually be found in different kinds
of reference books. But often they call up a tradition, and then the necessary information can only be had from experience. "Proud Maisie" (p. 38)
and "La Belle Dame sans Merci" (p. 54), for instance, *allude* to the tradition of the folk ballad. Auden's "As I Walked Out One Evening" (p. 130)
alludes jokingly to the tradition of love poetry in which fantastic claims
are made about the longevity of the lover's faithfulness. Shakespeare's
"Sonnet 130" (p. 126) alludes to the tradition of the "blazon of beauty,"
which is a lover's description of the several beauties of his loved one from
the crown of her pretty head right down to her charming toes. Kenneth
Patchen's "In Order To" (p. 125) alludes to the type of folk tale in which
the hero has to perform all sorts of impossible feats in order to win the
king's daughter. For these matters there's no dictionary and can be none.
As we have to learn about baseball by watching it, we have to learn about
literature by reading it.

iii

Two further forms of comparison to be considered here are *juxtaposition*
and *pun*. *Juxtaposition* is a comparison achieved by simply placing the
names of objects side by side—in other words, juxtaposing them, in such
a way as to imply that the listener or reader should look for a connection.
When Pope, for example, writes of midday in "The Rape of the Lock"
(I, 15–16) and says:

> Now lap dogs give themselves the rousing shake,
> And sleepless lovers, just at twelve, awake:

we can look beyond the comic paradox of the "sleepless lovers" who
awake at noon to see that the juxtaposition of "lap dogs" and "lovers" is
an implied comparison, for the context has already made it clear that in

the world this poem describes—the world of fashionable gentlemen-about-town, who have nothing to do but pay compliments to pretty debutantes—lovers and lap dogs can hardly be distinguished from each other. Ransom, similarly, in "Piazza Piece" (p. 40) implies a comparison by juxtaposing the lady's beauty, the roses on her trellis, and the moon—three things that fade. Gray, at the close of the first stanza of "Elegy Written in a Country Churchyard"(p.103), manages to imply a connection between the falling darkness and the melancholy quiet of the speaker by juxtaposing "darkness" and "me." The great virtue of juxtaposition, as these instances show, is that it's unobtrusive. One may make a witty comparison this way (lap dogs and lovers) without calling attention to one's wittiness, or a sober comparison (darkness and me) without falling into the self-consciousness of "The darkness of the evening is my darkness."

Puns are familiar enough to all of us, but not everyone knows how wide their range is or to what heights of meaning they may rise. At the bottom of their range, we have of course the "execrable pun," the kind which has given the whole species a bad odor: "Why did the moron throw himself from the Hotel Astor? Because he wanted to make a hit on Broadway." At the top of its range, on the other hand, we have on one side the genuinely witty pun, as in this example, "A Happy Time":

> There was a young fellow named Hall,
> Who fell in the spring in the fall;
> 'Twould have been a sad thing
> If he'd died in the spring,
> But he didn't—he died in the fall.   5
>
> —*A Happy Time*
> ANONYMOUS

and on the other side, still at the top, the deeply serious pun, which often compresses into a single word the struggle of two passions, two ideas, two ideals, or even two different worlds. In Shakespeare's *Hamlet,* the young prince, shocked by the corruption he has found in his mother and the knowledge that his father was murdered by his uncle, comes upon Ophelia, the woman he loves, praying. Her apparent innocence and purity as he contemplates her, together with his new-found knowledge of the evil the world contains, leads him to exclaim in a rush of desire to protect her: "Get thee to a nunnery." Later in the scene he discovers that Ophelia's father and his uncle, the murderous king, are both spying on this interview and infers, rightly, that Ophelia, with her prayerbook, has been planted here by them. In a frenzy of anger at her willingness to betray him in this way, he associates her with all the vice of which he has so recently learned that women can be guilty, and now cries again, "Get thee to a nunnery." But the meaning this time is intensified by a pun. "Nunnery" was a slang term for a house of prostitution, and the punning use of this sense along with the other sense sums up and dramatizes for us Hamlet's anguish and bewilderment as he looks at her. If she is as innocent as she seems in her manner and her speech, then a nunnery is the place for her, to keep her from contamination in a vile world. But if she is as corrupt as she seems in having betrayed him, and as corrupt as his mother has proved to be, then a "nunnery"—in the base sense—is the place for her. This pun, one of the most moving in literature, indicates what meaning can be packed into a pun by one who knows how.

iv

Study the examples of allusion and pun in the following poems:

[3]   *There Was an Old Man of Dunoon*
                       ANONYMOUS

There was an old man of Dunoon
Who always ate soup with a fork.
   For he said: "As I eat
   Neither fish, fowl, nor flesh,
I should otherwise finish too quick."   5

[4]   *Epitaph on Newton*
                       ALEXANDER POPE (1688–1744)

Nature and Nature's laws lay hid in night:
God said, "Let Newton be!" and all was light.

CONSIDERATIONS

1 The point of poem 3 comes from the fact that it alludes to a well-known kind of poem. What is the kind? How does this poem differ from the kind? If all poems of this kind came to be written like the

one above, would the kind be more or less interesting? What does your conclusion indicate about the source of the main interest of the type?

2 Poem 4 makes two allusions. What are they?

3 There are puns in "night" and "light." Explain them.

[5]   *On His Blindness*

JOHN MILTON (1608–1674)

When I consider how my light is spent
Ere half my days in this dark world and wide,
And that one talent° which is death to hide
Lodged with me useless, though my soul more bent
To serve therewith my Maker, and present   5
My true account, lest He returning chide,
"Doth God exact day-labor, light denied?"
I fondly ask. But Patience, to prevent
That murmur, soon replies, "God doth not need
Either man's work or His own gifts.° Who best   10
Bear His mild yoke,° they serve Him best. His state
Is kingly: thousands° at His bidding speed,
And post o'er land and ocean without rest;
They also serve who only stand and wait." °

CONSIDERATIONS

1 In lines 1–8 Milton's speaker alludes to the New Testament parable of the talents. What is the speaker's own "talent"? Why does he fear it will now be "useless"?

°**talent:** See Matthew 25:14–30.   °**His own gifts:** the gifts God gives to men.
°**mild yoke:** Christ says in Matthew 11:30, ". . . my yoke is easy, and my burden is light."
°**thousands:** angels.
°**They . . . wait:** The reference here is also to angels; those who "serve" through meditation are of the highest order.

2 Since "useless" has the double sense here of "not usable" and "not yielding interest" ("use" can mean a return on one's money, as in the parable of the talents), it's a pun. "Light" in line 7 and "wait" in line 14 are also puns. Explain each.

3 What is compared to what by the metaphor in "spent" (line 1)? The metaphor in "exact day-labor" (line 7)? The metaphor in "yoke" (line 11)?

4 In the first eight lines the words "I," "me," "my" appear frequently. In the last six, these are replaced by "He," "His," "Him." Relate this fact to the change that the poem traces in the speaker's attitude.

[6]   *On First Looking into Chapman's*° *Homer*
         JOHN KEATS (1795–1821)

Much have I traveled in the realms of gold,
    And many goodly states and kingdoms seen;
    Round many western islands have I been
Which bards in fealty to Apollo hold.
Oft of one wide expanse had I been told   5
    That deep-browed Homer ruled as his demesne;
    Yet did I never breathe its pure serene
Till I heard Chapman speak out loud and bold:
Then felt I like some watcher of the skies
    When a new planet swims into his ken;   10
Or like stout Cortez° when with eagle eyes
    He stared at the Pacific—and all his men
Looked at each other with a wild surmise—
    Silent, upon a peak in Darien.°

°**Chapman:** George Chapman, Elizabethan playwright and poet who translated Homer.
°**Cortez:** leader in Spain's New World conquests; historically, Balboa discovered the Pacific.
°**Darien:** Panama.

CONSIDERATIONS

1 The speaker has "traveled" to "realms of gold," "goodly states and kingdoms," and "western islands," all of which refer physically to Europe and the New World (the Age of Discovery) but metaphorically (and that's what counts) to the great works of literature that the speaker has read. How is the metaphor carried through in relation to Homer? Be specific. What form of discovery is involved here?

2 What two activities are alluded to in the similes of the last six lines? How do these forms of discovery relate to the discovery dealt with in the first eight lines? How can it be said that the poem is developed around one major metaphor, with three different illustrations?

3 What do the choices for comparison show about Keats's attitude toward literature in general, and his particular feelings on discovering Homer through Chapman's translation?

[7]   *The Kingdom of God*
                    "In No Strange Land"

              FRANCIS THOMPSON (1860–1907)

O world invisible, we view thee,
O world intangible, we touch thee,
O world unknowable, we know thee,
Inapprehensible, we clutch thee!

Does the fish soar to find the ocean,   5
The eagle plunge to find the air—
That we ask of the stars in motion
If they have rumor of thee there?

Not where the wheeling systems° darken,
And our benumbed conceiving soars!—   10

°**wheeling systems:** the galaxies.

The drift of pinions,° would we hearken,
Beats at our own clay-shuttered doors.

The angels keep their ancient places;
Turn but a stone, and start a wing!
'Tis ye, 'tis your estrangèd faces,   15
That miss the many-splendored thing.

But, when so sad thou canst not sadder,
Cry;—and upon thy so sore loss
Shall shine the traffic of Jacob's ladder
Pitched betwixt Heaven and Charing Cross.°   20

Yea, in the night, my Soul, my daughter,
Cry,—clinging Heaven by the hems;
And lo, Christ walking on the water
Not of Gennesareth,° but Thames!°

CONSIDERATIONS

1 "Thee" in the first stanza refers, of course, to God. What paradoxes are raised in this stanza? How does the rest of the poem resolve them?

2 Why are the questions in lines 5–6 raised? How do they serve to answer themselves, and by extension to answer the question posed in lines 7–8 and expanded on in the third and fourth stanzas? Where are the angels' "ancient places"?

3 The title and subtitle allude to Luke 17:20–21 and Psalm 137:4. Line 19 alludes to Genesis 28:10–17; line 22 to Matthew 9:20–22 and 14:33–36; and lines 23–24 to Matthew 14:22–33. What part do these Biblical allusions play in the poem?

°**pinions:** wings.   °**Charing Cross:** section of London.   °**Gennesareth:** Sea of Galilee.   °**Thames:** river that flows through London.

[8]   *Kind of an Ode to Duty*

OGDEN NASH (1902–1971)

O Duty,
Why hast thou not the visage of a sweetie or a cutie?
Why glitter thy spectacles so ominously?
Why art thou clad so abominously?
Why art thou so different from Venus   5
And why do thou and I have so few interests mutually in common
    between us?
Why art thou fifty per cent martyr
And fifty-one per cent Tartar?

Why is it thy unfortunate wont
To try to attract people by calling on them either to leave undone
    the deeds they like, or to do the deeds they don't?   10
Why art thou so like an April postmortem
On something that died in the ortumn?
Above all, why dost thou continue to hound me?
Why are thou always albatrossly hanging around me?

Thou so ubiquitous,   15
And I so iniquitous.
I seem to be the one person in the world thou art perpetually
    preaching at who or to who;
Whatever looks like fun, there art thou standing between me and
    it, calling yoo-hoo.
O Duty, Duty!
How noble a man should I be hadst thou the visage of a sweetie
    or a cutie!   20
But as it is thou art so much forbiddinger than a Wodehouse hero's
    forbiddingest aunt
That in the words of the poet, When Duty whispers low, Thou
    must, this erstwhile youth replies, I just can't.

CONSIDERATIONS

An *ode* is a relatively long, complex, and serious poem. There have been odes to and on all kinds of abstractions: dejection, adversity, solitude, indolence, melancholy, and, of course, duty. Nash is obviously alluding to William Wordsworth's "Ode to Duty" and to odes in general. The first stanza of Wordsworth's "Ode" goes like this:

> Stern Daughter of the Voice of God!
> O Duty! if that name thou love,
> Who art a light to guide, a rod
> To check the erring, and reprove;
> Thou, who art victory and law   5
> When empty terrors overawe;
> From vain temptations dost set free;
> And calm'st the weary strife of frail humanity!

> —From *Ode to Duty*
> WILLIAM WORDSWORTH (1770–1850)

In other stanzas in the poem Wordsworth calls Duty "Stern Lawgiver" and "awful Power," but says that she wears "the Godhead's most benignant grace" and that he doesn't know "anything so fair/As is the smile upon thy face." Wordsworth wants to "serve more strictly," to be Duty's "Bondman," so that he can live in a "repose that ever is the same."

The poet referred to in the last line of Nash's poem is Ralph Waldo Emerson. Part III of Emerson's poem "Voluntaries" ends:

> When Duty whispers low, *thou must,*
> The youth replies, *I can.*

1 Nash's poem can be enjoyed without any knowledge of the foregoing information, but what does it gain by the allusions to the ode form itself and to Wordsworth's and Emerson's poems? What is the allusion in line 14 and how does it add to the poem's meaning? What is the pun in the phrase "hanging around"?

2 Why does the speaker wish Duty had the "visage of a sweetie or a cutie"? Why is "visage" a better word choice than "face" would be? (Look up the two words in a good dictionary; what special meaning does "visage" have?) What does Duty look like in this poem? What do you suppose "a Wodehouse hero's forbiddingest aunt" looks and acts

like? (P. G. Wodehouse is a modern British writer of humorous novels.)

3 Why does the speaker use such words as "hast thou" and "art"? What other language forms echo old-fashioned diction? With what do these words obviously contrast?

4 Why should this rightly be called a poem?

[9]   *Journey of the Magi*°
                  T. S. ELIOT (1888–1965)

"A cold coming we had of it,
Just the worst time of the year
For a journey, and such a long journey:
The ways deep and the weather sharp,
The very dead of winter." °   5
And the camels galled, sore-footed, refractory,
Lying down in the melting snow.
There were times we regretted
The summer palaces on slopes, the terraces,
And the silken girls bringing sherbet.   10
Then the camel men cursing and grumbling
And running away, and wanting their liquor and women,
And the night-fires going out, and the lack of shelters,
And the cities hostile and the towns unfriendly
And the villages dirty and charging high prices: 15
A hard time we had of it.
At the end we preferred to travel all night,
Sleeping in snatches,

°**Title:** See Matthew 2.
°**Lines 1–5:** The lines in quotation marks are adapted from a sermon by Bishop Lancelot Andrewes on Christmas Day, 1622: "It was no summer progress. A cold coming they had of it at this time of the year, just the worst time of the year to take a journey, and specially a long journey, in. The ways deep, the weather sharp, the days short, the sun farthest off, ... the very dead of winter."

With the voices singing in our ears, saying
That this was all folly.   20

Then at dawn we came down to a temperate valley,
Wet, below the snow line, smelling of vegetation;
With a running stream and a watermill beating the darkness,
And three trees° on the low sky,
And an old white horse° galloped away in the meadow.   25
Then we came to a tavern with vine-leaves over the lintel,
Six hands at the open door dicing for pieces of silver,°
And feet kicking the empty wine-skins.
But there was no information, and so we continued
And arrived at evening, not a moment too soon   30
Finding the place; it was (you may say) satisfactory.

All this was a long time ago, I remember,
And I would do it again, but set down
This set down
This: were we led all that way for   35
Birth or Death? There was a Birth, certainly,
We had evidence and no doubt. I had seen birth and death,
But had thought they were different; this Birth was
Hard and bitter agony for us, like Death, our death.
We returned to our places, these Kingdoms,   40
But no longer at ease here, in the old dispensation,
With an alien people clutching their gods.
I should be glad of another death.

°**three trees:** alludes to the three "trees" on Calvary.
°**white horse:** Revelation 6:2—"And I saw, and beheld a white horse: and
he that sat on him had a bow; and a crown was given unto him; and he
went forth conquering, and to conquer." See also Revelation 19:11–14.
°**dicing . . . silver:** reference to the casting of lots for Jesus's garments and
his betrayal for "thirty pieces of silver."

CONSIDERATIONS

1 What is the "subject" of this poem? Who are the Magi? What was their destination on this journey? What conditions did they meet with during its first phase (lines 1–20)? During its second phase (lines 21–31)? Why do you think the poet omits most of the third phase— the events surrounding their arrival? What was the effect on them when they returned home?

2 Who is the speaker of the poem? How far is he a well-defined personality, how far a voice? What do you take to be the situation he's responding to? What is his audience? Do you think he's talking to someone, writing to someone, or simply going over the experience in his mind? How would you describe the speaker's tone?

3 What type of foot recurs most frequently in the poem's rhythm? Does the poem have any recurrent sound pattern that functions in place of rhymes? What is it? To what extent does the rhythm of the third section combine the dominant rhythms of sections one and two?

4 a. At the climax of the journey (line 31) the poet uses understatement. Explain.
   b. What paradox having to do with birth and death appears in the poem's third section (lines 32–43)? What paradox having to do with being homeless at home?
   c. In the second section the speaker describes certain things that for him are only scenes remembered from the journey, but for us are Christian symbols—the three trees, the white horse, pieces of silver, the dicing. This is a form of irony. What form? Do you find irony of any sort elsewhere in the poem?
   d. What use is made of allusion in the poem?

5 Is the journey described in the poem simply a literal journey or is it a metaphor for something else? Could the two types of country the Magi go through represent kinds of experience which one must pass through but not linger in if one wishes to discover the Birth?

6 The journey's upshot is obviously discomfort after the return home. Then why does the speaker say he would do it again? Does the poem suggest there may be something wrong in being comfortable?

V

ADDITIONAL POEMS
CHRONOLOGICALLY
ARRANGED

Here are sixty-eight poems, arranged chronologically to cover some four hundred years of English and American poetry, and divided roughly between the premodern and modern periods. Lines from many of these poems have been used for illustrative purposes in previous sections of the book.

We have attempted to offer a wide range of poetry in this section. We hope that our choices will underscore those aspects of poetry examined earlier in the book. Although they vary in subject, treatment, and difficulty, they have in common readability and excellence.

The Three Ravens

ANONYMOUS

There were three ravens sat on a tree,
Downe a downe, hay downe, hay downe.
There were three ravens sat on a tree,
   With a downe.
There were three ravens sat on a tree,   5
They were as blacke as they might be.
   With a downe derrie, derrie, derrie, downe, downe.

The one of them said to his mate,
"Where shall we our breakfast take?"

"Downe in yonder greene field,
There lies a knight slain under his shield.

"His hounds they lie downe at his feete,
So well they can their master keepe.

"His haukes they flie so eagerly,
There's no fowle dare him come nie."° 15

Downe there comes a fallow doe,°
As great with yong as she might goe.

She lift up his bloudy hed,
And kist his wounds that were so red.

She got him up upon her backe, 20
And carried him to earthen lake.°

She buried him before the prime,°
She was dead herselfe ere evensong° time.

God send every gentleman,
Such haukes, such hounds, and such a leman.° 25

Barbara Allan
ANONYMOUS

It was in and about the Martinmas time,
    When the green leaves were a falling,
That Sir John Graeme, in the West Country,
    Fell in love with Barbara Allan.

He sent his man down through the town, 5
    To the place where she was dwelling:

°nie: nigh, near.   °fallow doe: See line 25.   °lake: pit.   °prime: early
morning worship.   °evensong: vespers; evening worship.   °leman:
sweetheart.

"O haste and come to my master dear,
 Gin ° ye be Barbara Allan."

O hooly,° hooly rose she up,
 To the place where he was lying,   **10**
And when she drew the curtain by,
 "Young man, I think you're dying."

"O it's I'm sick, and very, very sick,
 And 't is a' for Barbara Allan":
"O the better for me ye's never be,   **15**
 Tho your heart's blood were a spilling.

"O dinna ye mind,° young man," said she,
 "When ye was in the tavern a drinking,
That ye made the healths gae round and round,
 And slighted Barbara Allan?"   **20**

He turned his face unto the wall,
 And death was with him dealing:
"Adieu, adieu, my dear friends all,
 And be kind to Barbara Allan."

And slowly, slowly raise she up,
 And slowly, slowly left him,
And sighing said, she could not stay,
 Since death of life had reft ° him,

She had not gane a mile but twa,
 When she heard the dead-bell ringing, **30**
And every jow ° that the dead-bell gied, °
 It cry'd, Woe to Barbara Allan!

"O mother, mother, make my bed!
 O make it saft and narrow!
Since my love died for me to-day,   **35**
 I'll die for him to-morrow."

°**Gin:** if. °**hooly:** softly. °**mind:** remember. °**reft:** robbed. °**jow:**
toll. °**gied:** gave.

Sonnet 94
WILLIAM SHAKESPEARE (1564–1616)

They that have power to hurt and will do none,
That do not do the thing they most do show,°
Who, moving others, are themselves as stone,
Unmovèd, cold, and to temptation slow—
They rightly do inherit Heaven's graces   5
And husband nature's riches from expense.°
They are the lords and owners of their faces,
Others but stewards° of their excellence.
The summer's flower is to the summer sweet,
Though to itself it only live and die,   10
But if that flower with base infection meet,
The basest weed outbraves his dignity.°
   For sweetest things turn sourest by their deeds;
   Lilies that fester smell far worse than weeds.

Blow, Blow, Thou Winter Wind
From *As You Like It*, II, vii
WILLIAM SHAKESPEARE (1564–1616)

Blow, blow, thou winter wind.
Thou are not so unkind
   As man's ingratitude.
Thy tooth is not so keen,
Because thou art not seen,   5
   Although thy breath be rude.
Heigh-ho! Sing, heigh-ho! unto the green holly.
Most friendship is feigning, most loving mere folly.
   Then, heigh-ho, the holly!
     This life is most jolly.   10
Freeze, freeze, thou bitter sky,
That dost not bite so nigh

°**show:** show as possible. °**expense:** wasteful use. °**stewards:** servants, as opposed to "lords and owners." °**outbraves . . . dignity:** outdoes the flower.

As benefits forgot.
Though thou the waters warp,
Thy sting is not so sharp   15
As friend remembered not.
Heigh-ho! Sing, heigh-ho! unto the green holly.
Most friendship is feigning, most loving mere folly.
Then, heigh-ho, the holly!
This life is most jolly.   20

Go and Catch a Falling Star
JOHN DONNE (1572–1631)

Go and catch a falling star,
Get with child a mandrake° root,
Tell me where all past years are,
Or who cleft the devil's foot,
Teach me to hear mermaids° singing,   5
Or to keep off envy's stinging,
And find
What wind
Serves t' advance an honest° mind.

If thou be'st born to strange sights,   10
Things invisible to see,
Ride ten thousand days and nights
Till age snow° white hairs on thee;
Thou, when thou return'st, wilt tell me
All strange wonders that befell thee,   15
And swear
Nowhere
Lives a woman true, and fair.

If thou find'st one, let me know;
Such a pilgrimage were sweet;   20

°**mandrake:** an herb whose forked root resembles the human form.   °**mer-**
maids: the sirens.   °**honest:** chaste.   °**snow:** here a verb.

Yet do not, I would not go
 Though at next door we might meet.
Though she were true when you met her,
And last till you write your letter,
  Yet she
  Will be
False ere I come, to two or three.

25

A Hymn to God the Father

JOHN DONNE (1572–1631)

Wilt Thou forgive that sin where I begun,
 Which was my sin, though it were done before?
Wilt Thou forgive that sin, through which I run,
 And do run still, though still I do deplore?
  When Thou hast done, Thou hast not done,°   5
  For I have more.

Wilt Thou forgive that sin which I have won
 Others to sin, and made my sin their door?
Wilt Thou forgive that sin which I did shun
 A year, or two: but wallowed in a score?   10
  When Thou hast done, Thou hast not done,
  For I have more.

I have a sin of fear, that when I have spun
 My last thread, I shall perish on the shore;°
But swear by Thy self, that at my death Thy Son   15
 Shall shine as He shines now, and heretofore;
  And, having done that, Thou hast done;
  I fear no more.

°**done:** a pun on the poet's name.   °**perish ... shore:** have no afterlife.

Still to Be Neat

BEN JONSON (1572–1637)

Still to be neat, still to be dressed
As° you were going to a feast;
Still to be powdered, still perfumed:
Lady, it is to be presumed,
Though art's hid causes are not found,   5
All is not sweet, all is not sound.

Give me a look, give me a face
That makes simplicity a grace;
Robes loosely flowing, hair as free:
Such sweet neglect more taketh me   10
Than all th' adulteries of art;
They strike mine eyes, but not my heart.

Love

GEORGE HERBERT (1593–1633)

Love bade me welcome, yet my soul drew back,
 Guilty of dust and sin.
But quick-eyed Love, observing me grow slack
 From my first entrance in,
Drew nearer to me, sweetly questioning   5
 If I lackèd anything.

A guest, I answered, worthy to be here.
 Love said, You shall be he.
I, the unkind, the ungrateful? Ah, my dear,
 I cannot look on thee.   10
Love took my hand and smiling did reply,
 Who made the eyes but I?

°**as:** as if.

Truth, Lord, but I have marred them; let my shame
    Go where it doth deserve.
And know you not, says Love, who bore the blame?   15
    My dear, then I will serve.
You must sit down, says Love, and taste my meat.
    So I did sit and eat.

The Pulley°

GEORGE HERBERT (1593–1633)

When God at first made man,
Having a glass of blessings standing by,
Let us, said he, pour on him all we can.
Let the world's riches, which dispersèd lie,
    Contract into a span.   5

    So strength first made a way,
Then beauty flowed, then wisdom, honor, pleasure.
When almost all was out, God made a stay,
Perceiving that alone of all his treasure
    Rest in the bottom lay.   10

    For if I should, said he,
Bestow this jewel also on my creature,
He would adore my gifts instead of me,
And rest in nature, not the God of nature;
    So both should losers be.   15

    Yet let him keep the rest,
But keep them with repining restlessness.
Let him be rich and weary, that at least,
If goodness lead him not, yet weariness
    May toss him to my breast.   20

°**Title:** Be sure you know what a pulley is used for.

Go, Lovely Rose

EDMUND WALLER (1606–1687)

Go, lovely rose!
Tell her that wastes her time and me
   That now she knows,
When I resemble her to thee,
   How sweet and fair she seems to be.   5

   Tell her that's young
And shuns to have her graces spied,
   That hadst thou sprung
In deserts where no men abide,
   Thou must have uncommended died.   10

   Small is the worth
Of beauty from the light retired:
   Bid her come forth,
Suffer her self to be desired,
   And not blush so to be admired.   15

   Then die, that she
The common fate of all things rare
   May read in thee,
How small a part of time they share,
   That are so wondrous sweet and fair.   20

Why So Pale and Wan

SIR JOHN SUCKLING (1609–1642)

Why so pale and wan, fond lover?
   Prithee, why so pale?
Will, when looking well can't move her,
   Looking ill prevail?
   Prithee, why so pale?   5

Why so dull and mute, young sinner?
  Prithee, why so mute?
Will, when speaking well can't win her,
  Saying nothing do 't?
  Prithee, why so mute?   10

Quit, quit, for shame, this will not move,
  This cannot take her.
If of herself she will not love,
  Nothing can make her.
  The devil take her!   15

To Lucasta, Going to the Wars
RICHARD LOVELACE (1618–1658)

Tell me not, sweet, I am unkind,
  That from the nunnery
Of thy chaste breast and quiet mind,
  To war and arms I fly.

True, a new mistress now I chase,   5
  The first foe in the field;
And with a stronger faith embrace
  A sword, a horse, a shield.

Yet this inconstancy is such
  As you too shall adore;   10
I could not love thee, Dear, so much,
  Loved I not honor more.

To His Coy Mistress
ANDREW MARVELL (1621–1678)

Had we but world enough, and time,
This coyness, Lady, were no crime.

We would sit down, and think which way
To walk, and pass our long love's day.
Thou by the Indian Ganges' side   5
Shouldst rubies find: I by the tide
Of Humber° would complain. I would
Love you ten years before the Flood:
And you should, if you please, refuse
Till the conversion of the Jews.   10
My vegetable° love should grow
Vaster than empires, and more slow.
An hundred years should go to praise
Thine eyes, and on thy forehead gaze.
Two hundred to adore each breast: 15
But thirty thousand to the rest.
An age at least to every part,
And the last age should show your heart.
For, Lady, you deserve this state;°
Nor would I love at lower rate.°   20
    But at my back I always hear
Time's wingèd chariot hurrying near:
And yonder all before us lie
Deserts of vast eternity.
Thy beauty shall no more be found,   25
Nor, in thy marble vault, shall sound
My echoing song: then worms shall try°
That long preserved virginity:
And your quaint° honor turn to dust,
And into ashes all my lust.   30
The grave's a fine and private place,
But none, I think, do there embrace.
    Now therefore, while the youthful hue
Sits on thy skin like morning dew,

°**Humber:** estuary of the Trent and Ouse Rivers on the east coast of England,
the site of Hull, the city in which the poet lived. °**vegetable:** growing;
alive. °**state:** royal treatment. °**lower rate:** reference to value or cost.
°**try:** attempt (successfully). °**quaint:** prudish; old-maidish.

And while thy willing soul transpires°   35
At every pore with instant° fires,
Now let us sport us while we may;
And now, like am'rous birds of prey,
Rather at once our time devour,
Than languish in his slow-chapped° power.   40
Let us roll all our strength, and all
Our sweetness, up into one ball:
And tear our pleasures with rough strife,
Through the iron gates of life.
Thus, though we cannot make our sun   45
Stand still, yet we will make him run.

Ode on Solitude

ALEXANDER POPE (1688–1744)

Happy the man, whose wish and care
   A few paternal acres bound.
Content to breathe his native an,
       In his own ground.

Whose herds with milk, whose fields with bread,   5
   Whose flocks supply him with attire,
Whose trees in summer yield him shade,
       In winter fire.

Blest, who can unconcern'dly find
   Hours, days, and years slide soft away,   10
In health of body, peace of mind,
       Quiet by day,

Sound sleep by night; study and ease,
   Together mixed; sweet recreation;
And innocence, which most does please   15
       With meditation.

°**transpires:** breathes.   °**instant:** eager.   °**slow-chapped:** slow-jawed;
slow-devouring.

Thus let me live, unseen, unknown,
   Thus unlamented let me die,
Steal from the world, and not a stone
     Tell where I lie.   20

To a Young Heir
SAMUEL JOHNSON (1709–1784)

Long-expected one-and-twenty,
   Ling'ring year, at length is flown:
Pride and pleasure, pomp and plenty,
   Great * * * * * * *, are now your own.

Loosened from the minor's tether,   5
   Free to mortgage or to sell,
Wild as wind, and light as feather,
   Bid the sons of thrift farewell.

Call the Betsies, Kates, and Jennies,
   All the names that banish care;   10
Lavish of your grandsire's guineas,°
   Show the spirit of an heir.

All that prey on vice and folly
   Joy to see their quarry fly:
There the gamester, light and jolly,   15
   There the lender, grave and sly.

Wealth, my lad, was made to wander,
   Let it wander as it will;
Call the jockey,° call the pander,
   Bid them come and take their fill.   20

°**guineas:** coins now worth about $3.   °**jockey:** swindler.

When the bonny blade carouses,
   Pockets full, and spirits high—
What are acres? What are houses?
   Only dirt, or° wet or dry.

Should the guardian friend or mother   25
   Tell the woes of willful waste,
Scorn their counsel, scorn their pother;—°
   You can hang or drown at last!

The Tiger

WILLIAM BLAKE (1757–1827)

Tiger, Tiger, burning bright
In the forests of the night,
What immortal hand or eye
Could frame thy fearful symmetry?

In what distant deeps or skies   5
Burnt the fire of thine eyes?
On what wings dare he aspire?
What the hand dare seize the fire?

And what shoulder, and what art,
Could twist the sinews of thy heart?   10
And when thy heart began to beat,
What dread hand and what dread feet?

What the hammer? What the chain?
In what furnace was thy brain?
What the anvil? What dread grasp   15
Dare its deadly terrors clasp?

When the stars threw down their spears,
And watered heaven with their tears,

°**or:** either.   °**pother:** fussing.

Did He smile His work to see?
Did He who made the lamb make thee?   20

Tiger, Tiger, burning bright
In the forests of the night,
What immortal hand or eye
Dare frame thy fearful symmetry?

Mock On, Mock On, Voltaire, Rousseau
WILLIAM BLAKE (1757–1827)

Mock on, mock on, Voltaire,° Rousseau:°
Mock on, mock on; 'tis all in vain!
You throw the sand against the wind,
And the wind blows it back again.

And every sand becomes a gem   5
Reflected in the beams divine;
Blown back, they blind the mocking eye,
But still in Israel's paths they shine.

The atoms of Democritus°
And Newton's° particles of light   10
Are sands upon the Red Sea shore,
Where Israel's tents do shine so bright.

°**Voltaire:** pen name of François Marie Arouet (1694–1778), French philosopher and writer. All four men mentioned in the poem were, in Blake's eyes,
debunkers of faith or the spirit, as symbolized by the Israelites whom God
delivered out of bondage in Egypt (see the "Red Sea" reference in line
11).

°**Rousseau:** Jean Jacques Rousseau (1712–1778), French philosopher and
writer.

°**Democritus:** Greek scientific philosopher (460?–357? B.C.), who developed
one theory of atom behavior.

°**Newton:** Sir Isaac Newton (1642–1727), English scientific philosopher,
originator of the particle theory of light.

A Poison Tree

WILLIAM BLAKE (1757–1827)

I was angry with my friend:
I told my wrath, my wrath did end.
I was angry with my foe:
I told it not, my wrath did grow.

And I watered it in fears,   5
Night and morning with my tears:
And I sunnèd it with smiles,
And with soft deceitful wiles.

And it grew both day and night,
Till it bore an apple bright;   10
And my foe beheld it shine,
And he knew that it was mine,

And into my garden stole
When the night had veiled the pole:
In the morning glad I see   15
My foe outstretched beneath the tree.

And Did Those Feet in Ancient Time

WILLIAM BLAKE (1757–1827)

And did those feet in ancient time
Walk upon England's mountains green?°
And was the holy Lamb of God
On England's pleasant pastures seen?

And did the Countenance Divine   5
Shine forth upon our clouded hills?

°**And did . . . mountains green:** see Isaiah, 52:7.

And was Jerusalem builded here
Among these dark Satanic Mills?°

Bring me my Bow of burning gold:
Bring me my Arrows of desire: 10
Bring me my Spear: O clouds unfold!
Bring me my Chariot of fire.

I will not cease from Mental Fight,
Nor shall my Sword sleep in my hand
Till we have built Jerusalem°   15
In England's green and pleasant Land.

My Luve Is Like a Red, Red Rose
ROBERT BURNS (1759–1796)

O, my luve is like a red, red rose,
      That's newly sprung in June.
O my luve is like the melodie
      That's sweetly played in tune.

As fair art thou, my bonnie lass,   5
      So deep in luve am I,
And I will luve thee still, my dear,
      Till a'° the seas gang° dry.

Till a' the seas gang dry, my dear,
      And the rocks melt wi' the sun!   10
And I will luve thee still, my dear,
      While the sands o' life shall run.

°**Satanic Mills:** probably a reference to the grimy, inhuman factories of the early years of the Industrial Revolution.   °**Jerusalem:** i.e., the "New Jerusalem" of Biblical prophetic writing: the City of God on earth.   °**a':** all.   °**gang:** go.

And fare thee weel,° my only luve,
 And fare thee weel awhile!
And I will come again, my luve,   15
 Though it were ten thousand mile!

She Dwelt Among the Untrodden Ways
WILLIAM WORDSWORTH (1770–1850)

She dwelt among the untrodden ways
 Beside the springs of Dove,
A Maid whom there were none to praise
 And very few to love:

A violet by a mossy stone   5
 Half hidden from the eye!
—Fair as a star, when only one
 Is shining in the sky.

She lived unknown, and few could know
 When Lucy ceased to be;   10
But she is in her grave, and, oh,
 The difference to me!

A Slumber Did My Spirit Seal
WILLIAM WORDSWORTH (1770–1850)

A slumber did my spirit seal;
 I had no human fears:
She seemed a thing that could not feel
 The touch of earthly years.

°**weel:** well.
°**Dove:** name of a stream.

No motion has she now, no force;   5
   She neither hears nor sees;
Rolled round in earth's diurnal° course,
   With rocks, and stones, and trees.

The World Is Too Much With Us

WILLIAM WORDSWORTH (1770–1850)

The world is too much with us; late and soon,
Getting and spending, we lay waste our powers:
Little we see in Nature that is ours;
We have given our hearts away, a sordid boon!
This Sea that bares her bosom to the moon;   5
The winds that will be howling at all hours,
And are up-gathered now like sleeping flowers;
For this, for everything, we are out of tune;
It moves us not.—Great God! I'd rather be
A pagan suckled in a creed outworn;   10
So might I, standing on this pleasant lea,
Have glimpses that would make me less forlorn;
Have sight of Proteus° rising from the sea;
Or hear old Triton° blow his wreathèd horn.

°**diurnal:** daily.
°**Proteus:** Greek sea god, herdsman for Poseidon (Neptune). Proteus could change shape whenever he wished.
°**Triton:** another Greek sea god, son of Poseidon; he controlled the waves with his "wreathèd horn" (conch shell).

Kubla Khan

SAMUEL TAYLOR COLERIDGE (1772–1834)

In Xanadu° did Kubla Khan
   A stately pleasure-dome decree;
Where Alph, the sacred river, ran
   Through caverns measureless to man
Down to a sunless sea.   5
So twice five miles of fertile ground
With walls and towers were girdled round;
And here were gardens bright with sinuous rills
Where blossomed many an incense-bearing tree;
And here were forests ancient as the hills,   10
Enfolding sunny spots of greenery.

But O, that deep romantic chasm which slanted
Down the green hill athwart a cedarn cover!
A savage place! as holy and enchanted
As e'er beneath a waning moon was haunted   15
By woman wailing for her demon-lover!
And from this chasm, with ceaseless turmoil seething,
As if this earth in fast thick pants were breathing,
A mighty fountain momently was forced;
Amid whose swift, half-intermitted burst   20
Huge fragments vaulted like rebounding hail,
Or chaffy grain beneath the thresher's flail.

°**Xanadu:** As with "the sacred river" Alph (line 3), this is no real place, but simply any remote, exotic spot where the great Mongol emperor, Kubla Khan, could "decree" that a magnificent palace be built. The first 36 lines of the poem describe the wonder of Kubla Khan's "paradise" and the geyser that "momently" brings the sacred river to the surface. The last 18 lines play off against the first 36: the speaker ("I") will build a more magnificent "pleasure-dome" in the form of his artistic creation.

And 'mid these dancing rocks at once and ever
It flung up momently the sacred river.
Five miles meandering with a mazy motion   25
Through wood and dale the sacred river ran,
Then reached the caverns measureless to man,
And sank in tumult to a lifeless ocean;
And 'mid this tumult Kubla heard from far
Ancestral voices prophesying war!   30

    The shadow of the dome of pleasure
        Floated midway on the waves;
      Where was heard the mingled measure
        From the fountain and the caves.
It was a miracle of rare device,   35
A sunny pleasure-dome with caves of ice!

    A damsel with a dulcimer
        In a vision once I saw.
    It was an Abyssinian maid,
        And on her dulcimer she played,   40
    Singing of Mount Abora.
    Could I revive within me
      Her symphony and song,
To such a deep delight 'twould win me
That with music loud and long,   45
I would build that dome in air,
That sunny dome! those caves of ice!
And all who heard should see them there,
And all should cry, Beware! Beware!
His flashing eyes, his floating hair!   50
Weave a circle round him thrice,
    And close your eyes with holy dread,
    For he on honey-dew hath fed,
And drunk the milk of Paradise.

To Autumn

JOHN KEATS (1795–1821)

I

Season of mists and mellow fruitfulness,
    Close bosom-friend of the maturing sun;
Conspiring with him how to load and bless
    With fruit the vines that round the thatch-eaves run;
To bend with apples the mossed cottage-trees,   5
    And fill all fruit with ripeness to the core;
        To swell the gourd, and plump the hazel shells
    With a sweet kernel; to set budding more,
And still more, later flowers for the bees,
    Until they think warm days will never cease,   10
        For Summer has o'er-brimmed their clammy° cells.

II

Who hath not seen thee oft amid thy store?
    Sometimes whoever seeks abroad may find
Thee sitting careless on a granary floor,
    Thy hair soft-lifted by the winnowing wind;   15
Or on a half-reaped furrow sound asleep,
    Drowsed with the fume of poppies, while thy hook°
        Spares the next swath and all its twinèd flowers:
And sometimes like a gleaner thou dost keep
    Steady thy laden head across a brook;   20
    Or by a cider-press, with patient look,
        Thou watchest the last oozings hours by hours.

III

Where are the songs of Spring? Ay, where are they?
    Think not of them, thou hast thy music too,—
While barrèd clouds bloom the soft-dying day,   25
    And touch the stubble-plains with rosy hue;

°**clammy**: moist and sticky.   °**hook**: scythe.

Then in a wailful choir the small gnats mourn
　　Among the river sallows,° borne aloft
　　　　Or sinking as the light wind lives or dies;
And full-grown lambs loud bleat from hilly bourn;°   30
　　Hedge-crickets sing; and now with treble° soft
　　The red-breast whistles from a garden-croft;°
　　　　And gathering swallows twitter in the skies.

Ode on a Grecian Urn

JOHN KEATS (1795–1821)

Thou° still unravished bride of quietness,
　　Thou foster-child of silence and slow time,
Sylvan historian, who canst thus express°
　　A flowery tale more sweetly than our rhyme:
What leaf-fringed legend haunts about thy shape   5
　　Of deities or mortals, or of both,
　　　　In Tempe or the dales of Arcady?°
What men or gods are these? What maidens loth?
　　What mad pursuit? What struggle to escape?
　　　　What pipes and timbrels?° What wild ectasy?   10

Heard melodies are sweet, but those unheard°
　　Are sweeter; therefore, ye soft pipes, play on;
Not to the sensual ear, but, more endeared,
　　Pipe to the spirit ditties of no tone:
Fair youth, beneath the trees, thou canst not leave   15
　　Thy song, nor ever can those trees be bare;
　　　　Bold Lover, never, never canst thou kiss,
Though winning near the goal—yet, do not grieve;
　　She cannot fade, though thou hast not thy bliss,
　　　　For ever wilt thou love, and she be fair!   20

°**sallows**: willows.　°**bourn**: small stream.　°**treble**: high-pitched sound.
°**croft**: small, enclosed field.　°**Thou . . .**; the speaker is addressing the
decorated urn; the references in the poem reveal what is pictured on it.
°**express**: tell.　°**Tempe . . . Arcady**: valleys in Greece, highly idealized.
°**timbrels**: tambourines.　°**unheard**: i.e., imagined.

Ah, happy, happy boughs! that cannot shed
    Your leaves, nor ever bid the spring adieu;
And, happy melodist, unwearièd,
    For ever piping songs for ever new;
More happy love! more happy, happy love!   25
    For ever warm and still to be enjoyed,
        For ever panting, and for ever young;
All breathing human passion far above,
    That leaves a heart high-sorrowful and cloyed,
        A burning forehead, and a parching tongue.   30

Who are these coming to the sacrifice?
    To what green altar, O mysterious priest,
Lead'st thou that heifer lowing at the skies,
    And all her silken flanks with garlands dressed?
What little town by river or sea shore,   35
    Or mountain-built with peaceful citadel,
        Is emptied of this folk, this pious morn?
And, little town, thy streets for evermore
    Will silent be; and not a soul to tell
        Why thou art desolate, can e'er return.   40

O Attic° shape! Fair attitude! with brede°
    Of marble men and maidens overwrought,
With forest branches and the trodden weed;
    Thou, silent form, dost tease us out of thought
As doth eternity:° Cold Pastoral!   45
    When old age shall this generation waste,
        Thou shalt remain, in midst of other woe
Than ours, a friend to man, to whom thou say'st,
    "Beauty is truth, truth beauty,"—that is all
        Ye know on earth, and all ye need to know.   50

°**Attic:** region of Greece; Athens was its capital.   °**brede:** embroidery, ornamentation.   °**eternity:** i.e., the idea of eternity.

My Last Duchess
ROBERT BROWNING (1812–1889)

That's my last Duchess painted on the wall,
Looking as if she were alive. I call
That piece a wonder, now: Frà Pandolf's ° hands
Worked busily a day, and there she stands.
Will 't please you sit and look at her? I said   5
"Frà Pandolf" by design, for never read
Strangers like you that pictured countenance,
The depth and passion of its earnest glance,
But to myself they turned (since none puts by
The curtain I have drawn for you, but I)   10
And seemed as they would ask me, if they durst,°
How such a glance came there; so, not the first
Are you to turn and ask thus. Sir, 'twas not
Her husband's presence only, called that spot
Of joy into the Duchess' cheek: perhaps   15
Frà Pandolf chanced to say, "Her ° mantle laps
Over my lady's wrist too much," or "Paint
Must never hope to reproduce the faint
Half-flush that dies along her throat": such stuff
Was courtesy, she thought, and cause enough   20
For calling up that spot of joy. She had
A heart—how shall I say?—too soon made glad,
Too easily impressed; she liked whate'er
She looked on, and her looks went everywhere.
Sir, 'twas all one! My favor ° at her breast,   25
The dropping of the daylight in the West,
The bough of cherries some officious fool

°**Frà Pandolf**: name of the (imaginary) Renaissance artist who painted the
portrait.
°**durst**: dared.
°**Her**: the artist uses the third person form as a mark of deference to nobility.
°**favor**: i.e., gift.

Broke in the orchard for her, the white mule
She rode with round the terrace—all and each
Would draw from her alike the approving speech,　30
Or blush, at least. She thanked men,—good!
　　but thanked
Somehow—I know not how—as if she ranked
My gift of a nine-hundred-years-old name
With anybody's gift. Who'd stoop to blame
This sort of trifling? Even had you skill　35
In speech—(which I have not)—to make your will
Quite clear to such an one, and say, "Just this
Or that in you disgusts me; here you miss,
Or there exceed the mark"—and if she let
Herself be lessoned so, nor plainly set　40
Her wits to yours, forsooth, and made excuse,
—E'en then would be some stooping; and I choose
Never to stoop. Oh sir, she smiled, no doubt,
Whene'er I passed her; but who passed without
Much the same smile? This grew; I gave commands;　45
Then all smiles stopped together. There she stands
As if alive. Will 't please you rise? We'll meet
The company below, then. I repeat,
The Count your master's known munificence
Is ample warrant that no just pretense　50
Of mine for dowry will be disallowed;
Though his fair daughter's self, as I avowed
At starting, is my object. Nay, we'll go
Together down, sir. Notice Neptune,° though,
Taming a sea-horse, thought a rarity,　55
Which Claus of Innsbruck ° cast in bronze for me!

°**Neptune:** the sea-god.
°**Claus of Innsbruck:** another imaginary Renaissance artist.

Dover Beach

MATTHEW ARNOLD (1822–1888)

The sea is calm tonight,
The tide is full, the moon lies fair
Upon the Straits;—on the French coast, the light
Gleams, and is gone; the cliffs of England° stand,
Glimmering and vast, out in the tranquil bay.   5
Come to the window, sweet is the night air!
Only, from the long line of spray
Where the sea meets the moon-blanched sand,
Listen! you hear the grating roar
Of pebbles which the waves suck back, and fling,   10
At their return, up the high strand,
Begin, and cease, and then again begin,
With tremulous cadence slow, and bring
The eternal note of sadness in.

Sophocles° long ago   15
Heard it on the Aegean, and it brought
Into his mind the turbid ebb and flow
Of human misery; we
Find also in the sound a thought,
Hearing it by this distant northern sea.   20

The sea of faith
Was once, too, at the full, and round earth's shore
Lay like the folds of a bright girdle° furled;
But now I only hear
Its melancholy, long, withdrawing roar,   25

°**cliffs of England:** the Dover chalk cliffs.
°**Sophocles:** Greek dramatist; in *Antigone* he has the chorus associate man's
lot with "a wave cresting out of the black northeast,/When the long darkness under sea roars up/And bursts drumming death upon the wind-
whipped sand." (Translation of Dudley Fitts and Robert Fitzgerald.)
°**girdle:** sash.

Retreating to the breath
Of the night-wind down the vast edges drear
And naked shingles° of the world.

    Ah, love, let us be true
To one another! for the world, which seems   30
To lie before us like a land of dreams,
So various, so beautiful, so new,
Hath really neither joy, nor love, nor light,
Nor certitude, nor peace, nor help for pain;
And we are here as on a darkling plain   35
Swept with confused alarms of struggle and flight,
Where ignorant armies clash by night.

I Like to See It Lap the Miles

EMILY DICKINSON (1830–1886)

I like to see it lap the miles,
And lick the valleys up,
And stop to feed itself at tanks;
And then, prodigious, step

Around a pile of mountains,   5
And, supercilious, peer
In shanties by the sides of roads;
And then a quarry pare

To fit its ribs, and crawl between,
Complaining all the while   10
In horrid, hooting stanza;
Then chase itself down hill

°shingles: gravel beaches.

And neigh like Boanerges;°
Then, punctual as a star,
Stop—docile and omnipotent—   15
At its own stable door.

I Heard a Fly Buzz When I Died
EMILY DICKINSON (1830–1886)

I heard a fly buzz when I died;
  The stillness in the room
Was like the stillness in the air
  Between the heaves of storm.

The eyes around had wrung them dry,   5
  And breaths were gathering firm
For that last onset, when the king
  Be witnessed in the room.

I willed my keepsakes, signed away
  What portion of me be   10
Assignable,—and then it was
  There interposed a fly,

With blue, uncertain, stumbling buzz,
  Between the light and me;
And then the windows failed, and then   15
  I could not see to see.

After Great Pain a Formal Feeling Comes
EMILY DICKINSON (1830–1886)

After great pain a formal feeling comes—
The nerves sit ceremonious like tombs;

°**Boanerges:** "sons of thunder," name applied by Jesus to the sons of Zebe-
dee, James and John, who wanted to destroy the Samaritans with fire from
heaven.

The stiff heart questions—was it He that bore?
And yesterday—or centuries before?

The feet mechanical go round   5
A wooden way
Of ground or air or ought,
Regardless grown,
A quartz contentment like a stone.

This is the hour of lead   10
Remembered if outlived
As freezing persons recollect
The snow—
First chill, then stupor, then
The letting go.   15

God's Grandeur

GERARD MANLEY HOPKINS (1844–1889)

The world is charged with the grandeur of God.
    It will flame out, like shining from shook foil;°
    It gathers to a greatness, like the ooze of oil°
Crushed. Why do men then now not reck his rod?°
Generations have trod, have trod, have trod;   5
    And all is seared with trade; bleared, smeared with toil;
    And wears man's smudge and shares man's smell: the soil
Is bare now, nor can foot feel, being shod.

And for° all this, nature is never spent;°
    There lives the dearest freshness deep down things;   10
And though the last lights off the black West went
    Oh, morning, at the brown brink eastward, springs—
Because the Holy Ghost over the bent
    World broods with warm breast and with ah! bright wings.

°**foil:** thin sheetmetal.   °**ooze of oil:** from pressed olives.   °**reck his rod:** concern themselves about God's punishment.   °**for:** in spite of.   °**spent:** used up; exhausted.

Spring and Fall:
To a Young Child

GERARD MANLEY HOPKINS (1844–1889)

Márgarét,° are you grieving
Over Goldengrove unleaving?°
Leáves, líke the things of man, you
With your fresh thoughts care for, can you?
Áh! Ás the heart grows older   5
It will come to such sights colder
By and by, nor spare a sigh
Though worlds of wanwood leafmeal° lie;
And yet you wíll weep and know why.
Now no matter, child, the name: 10
Sórrow's spríngs áre the same.
Nor mouth had, no nor mind, expressed
What heart heard of, ghost guessed:
It ís the blight man was born for,
It is Margaret you mourn for.   15

Thou Art Indeed Just, Lord°

GERARD MANLEY HOPKINS (1844–1889)

Justus quidem tu es, Domine, si disputem tecum: verum-tamen justa
loquar ad te: Quare via impiorum prosperatur? &c.

Thou art indeed just, Lord, if I contend
With thee; but, sir, so what I plead is just.
Why do sinners' ways prosper? and why must
Disappointment all I endeavour end?
Wert thou my enemy, O thou my friend,   5
How wouldst thou worse, I wonder, than thou dost
Defeat, thwart me? Oh, the sots and thralls of lust

°**Márgarét:** The special stress marks are Hopkins's. Some syllables that
would not normally get stress are purposely given stress.
°**unleaving:** losing its leaves.   °**leafmeal:** like "piecemeal."
°**Title:** Jeremiah 12:1; the first three lines of the poem provide the translation for the Latin.

Do in spare hours more thrive than I that spend,
Sir, life upon thy cause. See, banks and brakes
Now, leavèd how thick! lacèd they are again 　　10
With fretty chervil, look, and fresh wind shakes
Them; birds build—but not I build; no, but strain,
Time's eunuch, and not breed one work that wakes.
Mine, O thou lord of life, send my roots rain.

On Wenlock Edge°
A. E. HOUSMAN (1859–1936)

On Wenlock Edge the wood's in trouble;
　　His forest fleece the Wrekin heaves;
The gale, it plies the saplings double,
　　And thick on Severn snow the leaves.

'Twould blow like this through holt° and hanger° 　　5
　　When Uricon the city stood:
'Tis the old wind in the old anger,
　　But then it threshed another wood.

Then, 'twas before my time, the Roman
　　At yonder heaving hill would stare: 　　10
The blood that warms an English yeoman,
　　The thoughts that hurt him, they were there.

There, like the wind through woods in riot,
　　Through him the gale of life blew high;
The tree of man was never quiet: 　　15
　　Then 'twas the Roman, now 'tis I.

°**Title:** The places named in the poem are all in Shropshire, England. Uricon was an old Roman town where Wenlock now stands. The Wrekin is a wooded hill near the town; Wenlock Edge is a ridge nearby, and the Severn is a river.
°**holt:** a small woods on a steep slope.　　°**hanger:** essentially the same thing.

The gale, it plies the saplings double,
    It blows so hard, 'twill soon be gone:
Today the Roman and his trouble
    Are ashes under Uricon.   20

1887°

A. E. HOUSMAN (1859–1936)

From Clee° to heaven the beacon° burns,
    The shires have seen it plain,
From north and south the sign returns
    And beacons burn again.

Look left, look right, the hills are bright,   5
    The dales are light between,
Because 'tis fifty years tonight
    That God has saved the Queen.°

Now, when the flame they watch not towers
    About the soil they trod,   10
Lads, we'll remember friends of ours
    Who shared the work with God.

To skies that knit their heartstrings right,
    To fields that bred them brave,
The saviors come not home tonight: 15
    Themselves they could not save.

It dawns in Asia, tombstones show
    And Shropshire names are read;

°**Title:** In 1887 Victoria celebrated her fiftieth year as Queen of England.
°**Clee:** town in Shropshire, a county in the west of England on the Welsh border.
°**beacon:** Beacons were lighted up and down the land to celebrate the Queen's anniversary.
°**God . . . Queen:** See line 25.

And the Nile spills his overflow
    Beside the Severn's° dead.   20

We pledge in peace by farm and town
    The Queen they served in war,
And fire the beacons up and down
    The land they perished for.

"God save the Queen" we living sing,   25
    From height to height 'tis heard;
And with the rest your voices ring,
    Lads of the Fifty-third.°

Oh, God will save her, fear you not:
    Be you the men you've been,   30
Get you the sons your fathers got,
    And God will save the Queen.

To a Friend Whose Work Has Come to Nothing

WILLIAM BUTLER YEATS (1865–1939)

Now all the truth is out,
Be secret and take defeat
From any brazen throat,
For how can you compete,
Being honor bred, with one   5
Who, were it proved he lies,
Were neither shamed in his own
Nor in his neighbors' eyes?
Bred to a harder thing
Than Triumph, turn away,   10
And like a laughing string
Whereon mad fingers play
Amid a place of stone,

°**Severn:** Shropshire river.   °**Fifty-third:** Shropshire regiment.

Be secret and exult,
Because of all things known   15
That is most difficult.

The Wild Swans at Coole°
WILLIAM BUTLER YEATS (1865–1939)

The trees are in their autumn beauty,
The woodland paths are dry,
Under the October twilight the water
Mirrors a still sky;
Upon the brimming water among the stones   5
Are nine-and-fifty swans.

The nineteenth autumn has come upon me
Since I first made my count;
I saw, before I had well finished,
All suddenly mount   10
And scatter wheeling in great broken rings
Upon their clamorous wings.

I have looked upon those brilliant creatures,
And now my heart is sore.
All's changed since I, hearing at twilight,   15
The first time on this shore,
The bell-beat of their wings above my head,
Trod with a lighter tread.

Unwearied still, lover by lover,
They paddle in the cold   20
Companionable streams or climb the air;
Their hearts have not grown old;
Passion or conquest, wander where they will,
Attend upon them still.

°**Title:** Coole, in Galway, Ireland, was the home of Yeats's friend, Lady
Gregory; he spent many summers and early falls there (see line 7).

But now they drift on the still water   25
Mysterious, beautiful;
Among what rushes will they build,
By what lake's edge or pool
Delight men's eyes when I awake some day
To find they have flown away?   30

Vacillation
IV

WILLIAM BUTLER YEATS (1865–1939)

My fiftieth year had come and gone,
I sat, a solitary man,
In a crowded London shop,
An open book and empty cup
On the marble table-top.   5
While on the shop and street I gazed
My body of a sudden blazed;
And twenty minutes more or less
It seemed, so great my happiness,
That I was blessèd and could bless.   10

Acquainted with the Night
ROBERT FROST (1874–1963)

I have been one acquainted with the night.
I have walked out in rain—and back in rain.
I have outwalked the furthest city light.

I have looked down the saddest city lane.
I have passed by the watchman on his beat   5
And dropped my eyes, unwilling to explain.

I have stood still and stopped the sound of feet
When far away an interrupted cry
Came over houses from another street,

But not to call me back or say good-bye;   10
And further still at an unearthly height,
One luminary clock against the sky

Proclaimed the time was neither wrong nor right.
I have been one acquainted with the night.

Desert Places
ROBERT FROST (1874–1963)

Snow falling and night falling fast oh fast
In a field I looked into going past,
And the ground almost covered smooth in snow,
But a few weeds and stubble showing last.

The woods around it have it—it is theirs.   5
All animals are smothered in their lairs.
I am too absent-spirited to count;
The loneliness includes me unawares.

And lonely as it is that loneliness
Will be more lonely ere it will be less—   10
A blanker whiteness of benighted snow
With no expression, nothing to express.

They cannot scare me with their empty spaces
Between stars—on stars where no human race is.
I have it in me so much nearer home   15
To scare myself with my own desert places.

archy confesses °
DON MARQUIS (1879–1937)

coarse
jocosity
catches the crowd

°The speaker here, archy, is a cockroach who writes poems on a typewriter
by jumping from key to key. Given the nature of typewriters, he can't make
capital letters or certain punctuation marks, but neither is necessary.

shakespeare
and i
are often
low browed

the fish wife
curse
and the laugh
of the horse
shakespeare
and i
are frequently
coarse
aesthetic
excuses
in bill s behalf
are adduced
to refine
big bill s
coarse laugh

but bill
he would chuckle
to hear such guff
he pulled
rough stuff
and he liked
rough stuff

hoping you
are the same
                archy

Preludes

T. S. ELIOT (1888–1965)

I

The winter evening settles down
With smell of steaks in passageways.
Six o'clock.
The burnt-out ends of smoky days.
And now a gusty shower wraps   5
The grimy scraps
Of withered leaves about your feet
And newspapers from vacant lots;
The showers beat
On broken blinds and chimney pots,   10
And at the corner of the street
A lonely cab-horse steams and stamps.
And then the lighting of the lamps.

II

The morning comes to consciousness
Of faint stale smells of beer   15
From the sawdust-trampled street
With all its muddy feet that press
To early coffee-stands.
With the other masquerades
That time resumes,   20
One thinks of all the hands
That are raising dingy shades
In a thousand furnished rooms.

III

You tossed a blanket from the bed,
You lay upon your back, and waited;   25
You dozed, and watched the night revealing
The thousand sordid images
Of which your soul was constituted;

They flickered against the ceiling.
And when all the world came back 30
And the light crept up between the shutters
And you heard the sparrows in the gutters,
You had such a vision of the street
As the street hardly understands;
Sitting along the bed's edge, where 35
You curled the papers from your hair,
Or clasped the yellow soles of feet
In the palms of both soiled hands.

IV

His soul stretched tight across the skies
That fade behind a city block, 40
Or trampled by insistent feet
At four and five and six o'clock;
And short square fingers stuffing pipes,
And evening newspapers, and eyes
Assured of certain certainties, 45
The conscience of a blackened street
Impatient to assume the world.

I am moved by fancies that are curled
Around these images, and cling:
The notion of some infinitely gentle 50
Infinitely suffering thing.

Wipe your hand across your mouth, and laugh;
The worlds revolve like ancient women
Gathering fuel in vacant lots.

The End of the World
ARCHIBALD MACLEISH (1892–1982)

Quite unexpectedly, as Vasserot
The armless ambidextrian was lighting

A match between his great and second toe,
And Ralph the lion was engaged in biting
The neck of Madame Sossman while the drum   5
Pointed, and Teeny was about to cough
In waltz-time swinging Jocko by the thumb—
Quite unexpectedly the top blew off:
And there, there overhead, there, there hung over
Those thousands of white faces, those dazed eyes,   10
There in the starless dark the poise, the hover,
There with vast wings across the cancelled skies,
There in the sudden blackness the black pall
Of nothing, nothing, nothing—nothing at all.

Arms and the Boy°
WILFRED OWEN (1893–1918)

Let the boy try° along this bayonet-blade
How cold steel is, and keen with hunger of blood;
Blue with all malice, like a madman's flash;
And thinly drawn with famishing for flesh.

Lend him to stroke these blind, blunt bullet-heads   5
Which long to nuzzle in the hearts of lads,
Or give him cartridges of fine zinc teeth,
Sharp with the sharpness of grief and death.
For his teeth seem for laughing round an apple.
There lurk no claws behind his fingers supple;   10
And God will grow no talons at his heels,
Nor antlers through the thickness of his curls.
someones married their everyones
laughed their cryings and did their dance
(sleep wake hope and then) they
said their nevers they slept their dream   20

°**Title:** There is ironic reference here to the opening words of Virgil's great
epic, the *Aeneid:* "Arms and the man I sing."
°**try:** prove by feeling.

Anyone Lived in a Pretty How Town

E. E. CUMMINGS (1894–1962)

anyone lived in a pretty how town
(with up so floating many bells down)
spring summer autumn winter
he sang his didn't he danced his did.

Women and men (both little and small)   5
cared for anyone not at all
they sowed their isn't they reaped their same
sun moon stars rain

children guessed (but only a few
and down they forgot as up they grew   10
autumn winter spring summer)
that noone loved him more by more

when by now and tree by leaf
she laughed his joy she cried his grief
bird by snow and stir by still   15
anyone's any was all to her

someones married their everyones
laughed their cryings and did their dance
(sleep wake hope and then) they
said their nevers they slept their dream   20

stars rain sun moon
(and only the snow can begin to explain
how children are apt to forget to remember
with up so floating many bells down)

one day anyone died i guess   25
(and noone stooped to kiss his face)
busy folk buried them side by side
little by little and was by was

all by all and deep by deep
and more by more they dream their sleep   30
noone and anyone earth by april
wish by spirit and if by yes.

Women and men (both dong and ding)
summer autumn winter spring
reaped their sowing and went their came   35
sun moon stars rain

Before Disaster
YVOR WINTERS (1900–1968)

Evening traffic homeward burns,
Swift and even on the turns,
Drifting weight in triple rows,
Fixed relation and repose.
This one edges out and by,   5
Inch by inch with steady eye.
But should error be increased,
Mass and moment are released;
Matter loosens, flooding blind,
Levels driver to its kind.   10

   Ranks of nations thus descend,
Watchful to a stormy end.
By a moment's calm beguiled,
I have got a wife and child.
Fool and scoundrel guide the State.   15
Peace is whore to Greed and Hate.
Nowhere may I turn to flee:
Action is security.
Treading change with savage heel,
We must live or die by steel.   20

Only the Polished Skeleton
COUNTEE CULLEN (1903–1946)

The heart has need of some deceit
   To make its pistons rise and fall;

For less than this it would not beat,
    Nor flush the sluggish vein at all.

With subterfuge and fraud the mind   5
    Must fend and parry thrust for thrust,
With logic brutal and unkind
    Beat off the onslaughts of the dust.

Only the polished skeleton,
    Of flesh relieved and pauperized,   10
Can rest at ease and think upon
    The worth of all it so despised.

The Fury of Aerial Bombardment

RICHARD EBERHART (1904–   )

You would think the fury of aerial bombardment
Would rouse God to relent; the infinite spaces
Are still silent. He looks on shock-pried faces.
History, even, does not know what is meant.

You would feel that after so many centuries   5
God would give man to repent; yet he can kill
As Cain could, but with multitudinous will,
No farther advanced than in his ancient furies.°

Was man made stupid to see his own stupidity?
Is God by definition indifferent, beyond us all?   10
Is the eternal truth man's fighting soul
Wherein the Beast° ravens° in its own avidity?°

Of Van Wettering I speak, and Averill,
Names on a list, whose faces I do not recall

°**furies:** the avenging spirits of classical mythology.
°**Beast:** reference to Revelations 13:18, which applies the term to any vicious
ruler or warrior.
°**ravens:** greedily eats.   °**avidity:** uncontrollable greed.

But they are gone to early death, who late in school   15
Distinguished the belt feed lever from the belt holding pawl.°

New Hampshire, February
RICHARD EBERHART (1904–   )

Nature had made them hide in crevices,
Two wasps so cold they looked like bark.
Why I do not know, but I took them
And I put them
In a metal pan, both day and dark.   5

Like God touching his finger to Adam
I felt, and thought of Michelangelo,
For whenever I breathed on them,
The slightest breath,
They leaped, and preened as if to go.   10

My breath controlled them always quite.
Mor sensitive than electric sparks
They came into life
Or they withdrew to ice,
While I watched, suspending remarks.   15

Then one in a blind career got out,
And fell to the kitchen floor. I
Crushed him with my cold ski boot,
By accident. The other
Had not the wit to try or die.   20

And so the other is still my pet.
The moral of this is plain.
But I will shirk it.
You will not like it. And
God does not live to explain.   25

°**belt . . . pawl:** machine-gun parts.

Musée des Beaux Arts

w. h. auden (1907–1973)

About suffering they were never wrong,
The Old Masters:° how well they understood
Its human position; how it takes place
While someone else is eating or opening a window or just walking
    dully along;
How, when the aged are reverently, passionately waiting   5
For the miraculous birth, there always must be
Children who did not specially want it to happen, skating
On a pond at the edge of the wood:
They never forgot
That even the dreadful martyrdom must run its course   10
Anyhow in a corner, some untidy spot
Where the dogs go on with their doggy life and the torturer's
    horse
Scratches its innocent behind on a tree.

In Brueghel's *Icarus,*° for instance: how everything turns away
Quite leisurely from the disaster; the ploughman may   15
Have heard the splash, the forsaken cry,
But for him it was not an important failure; the sun shone
As it had to on the white legs disappearing into the green
Water; and the expensive delicate ship that must have seen
Something amazing, a boy falling out of the sky,   20
Had somewhere to get to and sailed calmly on.

Conquistador

a. d. hope (1907–   )

I sing of the decline of Henry Clay
Who loved a white girl of uncommon size.
Although a small man in a little way,
He had in him some seed of enterprise.

°**Old Masters:** great painters of the sixteenth and seventeenth centuries.
°**Icarus:** "The Fall of Icarus," by the sixteenth-century Flemish painter,
Pieter Brueghel, one of the Old Masters.

Each day he caught the seven-thirty train   5
To work, watered his garden after tea,
Took an umbrella if it looked like rain
And was remarkably like you or me.

He had his hair cut once a fortnight, tried
Not to forget the birthday of his wife,   10
And might have lived unnoticed till he died
Had not ambition entered Henry's life.

He met her in the lounge of an hotel
—A most unusual place for him to go—
But there he was and there she was as well,   15
Sitting alone. He ordered beers for two.

She was so large a girl that when they came
He gave the waiter twice the usual tip.
She smiled without surprise, told him her name,
And as the name trembled on Henry's lip,   20

His parched soul, swelling like a desert root,
Broke out its delicate dream upon the air;
The mountains shook with earthquake under foot;
An angel seized him suddenly by the hair;

The sky was shrill with peril as he passed;   25
A hurricane crushed his senses with its din;
The wildlife crackled up his reeling mast;
The trumpet of a maelstrom sucked him in;

The desert shrivelled and burnt off his feet;
His bones and buttons an enormous snake   30
Vomited up; still in the shimmering heat
The pygmies showed him their forbidden lake

And then transfixed him with their poison darts;
He married six black virgins in a bunch,

Who, when they had drawn out his manly parts,   35
Stewed him and ate him lovingly for lunch.

Adventure opened wide its grisly jaws;
Henry looked in and knew the Hero's doom.
The huge white girl drank on without a pause
And, just at closing time, she asked him home.   40

The tram they took was full of Roaring Boys
Announcing the world's ruin and Judgment Day;
The sky blared with its grand orchestral voice
The Götterdämmerung of Henry Clay.

But in her quiet room they were alone.   45
There, towering over Henry by a head,
She stood and took her clothes off one by one,
And then she stretched herself upon the bed.

Her bulk of beauty, her stupendous grace
Challenged the lion heart in his puny dust.   50
Proudly his Moment looked him in the face:
He rose to meet it as a hero must;

Climbed the white mountain of unravished snow,
Planted his tiny flag upon the peak.
The smooth drifts, scarcely breathing, lay below.   55
She did not take the trouble to smile or speak.

And afterwards, it may have been in play,
The enormous girl rolled over and squashed him flat;
And, as she could not send him home that way,
Used him thereafter as a bedside mat.   60

Speaking at large, I will say this of her:
She did not spare expense to make him nice.
Tanned on both sides and neatly edged with fur,
The job would have been cheap at any price.

And when, in winter, getting out of bed,   65
Her large soft feet pressed warmly on the skin,
The two glass eyes would sparkle in his head,
The jaws extend their papier-mâché grin.

Good people, for the soul of Henry Clay
Offer your prayers, and view his destiny!   70
He was the Hero of our Time. He may
With any luck, one day, be you or me.

An Elementary School Classroom in a Slum
STEPHEN SPENDER (1909–   )

Far far from gusty waves these children's faces.
Like rootless weeds the torn hair round their paleness.
The tall girl with her weighed-down head. The paper-
Seeming boy with rat's eyes. The stunted unlucky heir
Of twisted bones, reciting a father's gnarled disease,   5
His lesson from his desk. At back of the dim class
One unnoted, mild and young: his eyes live in a dream
Of squirrels' game, in tree room, other than this.
On sour cream walls, donations. Shakespeare's head
Cloudless at dawn, civilized dome riding all cities.   10
Belled, flowery, Tyrolese valley. Open-handed map
Awarding the world its world. And yet, for these
Children, these windows, not this world, are world,
Where all their future's painted with a fog,
A narrow street sealed in with a lead sky,   15
Far far from rivers, capes, and stars of words.

Surely Shakespeare is wicked, the map a bad example
With ship and sun and love tempting them to steal—
For lives that slyly turn in their cramped holes
From fog to endless night? On their slag heap, these children   20
Wear skins peeped through by bones, and spectacles of steel
With mended glass, like bottle bits in slag.

Tyrol is wicked; map's promising a fable:
All of their time and space are foggy slum,
So blot their maps with slums as big as doom. 25

Unless, governor, teacher, inspector, visitor,
This map becomes their window and these windows
That open on their lives like crouching tombs
Break, O break open, till they break the town
And show the children to the fields and all their world 30
Azure on their sands, to let their tongues
Run naked into books, the white and green leaves open
The history theirs whose language is the sun.

To My Mother

GEORGE BARKER (1913–   )

Most near, most dear, most loved and most far,
Under the window where I often found her
Sitting as huge as Asia, seismic with laughter,
Gin and chicken helpless in her Irish hand,
Irresistible as Rabelais,° but most tender for 5
The lame dogs and hurt birds that surround her,—
She is a procession no one can follow after
But be like a little dog following a brass band.

She will not glance up at the bomber, or condescend
To drop her gin and scuttle to a cellar, 10
But lean on the mahogany table like a mountain
Whom only faith can move, and so I send
O all my faith and all my love to tell her
That she will move from mourning into morning.

° *Rabelais:* French Renaissance writer of an inexhaustible comic imagination.

Auto Wreck

KARL SHAPIRO (1913–   )

Its quick soft silver bell beating, beating,
And down the dark one ruby flare
Pulsing out red light like an artery,
The ambulance at top speed floating down
Past beacons and illuminated clocks   5
Wings in a heavy curve, dips down,
And brakes speed, entering the crowd.
The doors leap open, emptying light;
Stretchers are laid out, the mangled lifted
And stowed into the little hospital.   10
Then the bell, breaking the hush, tolls once,
And the ambulance with its terrible cargo
Rocking, slightly rocking, moves away,
As the doors, an afterthought, are closed.
We are deranged,° walking among the cops   15
Who sweep glass and are large and composed.
One is still making notes under the light.
One with a bucket douches ponds of blood
Into the street and gutter.
One hangs lanterns on the wrecks that cling,   20
Empty husks of locusts, to iron poles.

Our throats were tight as tourniquets,
Our feet were bound with splints, but now,
Like convalescents intimate and gauche,°
We speak through sickly smiles and warn   25
With the stubborn saw° of common sense,
The grim joke and the banal° resolution.
The traffic moves around with care,
But we remain, touching a wound

°**deranged:** unable to function properly; mentally confused.
°**gauche:** awkward.   °**saw:** a proverbial saying, like "Haste makes waste."
°**banal:** repeated so often as to be meaningless.

That opens to our richest horror.   30
Already old, the question Who shall die?
Becomes unspoken Who is innocent?
For death in war is done by hands;
Suicide has cause and stillbirth, logic;
And cancer, simple as a flower, blooms.   35
But this invites the occult° mind,
Cancels our physics° with a sneer,
And spatters all we knew of denouement°
Across the expedient and wicked stones.

The Dirty Word

KARL SHAPIRO (1913–   )

The dirty word hops in the cage of the mind like the Pondicherry vulture, stomping with its heavy left claw on the sweet meat of the brain and tearing it with its vicious beak, ripping and chopping the flesh. Terrified, the small boy bears the big bird of the dirty word into the house, and grunting, puffing, carries it up the stairs to his own room in the skull. Bits of black feather cling to his clothes and his hair as he locks the staring creature in the dark closet.

All day the small boy returns to the closet to examine and feed the bird, to caress and kick the bird, that now snaps and flaps its wings savagely whenever the door is opened. How the boy trembles and delights at the sight of the white excrement of the bird! How the bird leaps and rushes against the walls of the skull, trying to escape from the zoo of the vocabulary! How wildly snaps the sweet meat of the brain in its rage.

And the bird outlives the man, being freed at the man's death-funeral by a word from the rabbi.

(But I one morning went upstairs and opened the door and entered the closet and found in the cage of my mind the great bird dead. Softly

---

°**occult**: dealing with the supernatural.   °**physics**: reasoning power;·
scientific deduction.   °**denouement**: an outcome that is reasonable and logical.

I wept it and softly removed it and softly buried the body of the bird in the hollyhock garden of the house I lived in twenty years before. And out of the worn black feathers of the wing have I made these pens to write these elegies, for I have outlived the bird, and I have murdered it in my early manhood.)

A Refusal to Mourn the Death, by Fire, *of a Child in London*

DYLAN THOMAS (1914–1953)

Never° until the mankind making
Bird beast and flower
Fathering and all humbling darkness°
Tells° with silence the last light breaking
And the still hour   5
Is come of the sea tumbling in harness

And I must enter again the round
Zion° of the water bead°
And the synagogue° of the ear of corn
Shall I let pray the shadow of a sound°   10
Or sow my salt seed°
In the least valley of sackcloth° to mourn

The majesty and burning of the child's death.
I shall not murder

°**Never, etc.:** The sentence starting with "Never" goes to line 13: "Never ...Shall I (line 10) ... death."
°**Lines 1–3:** "Darkness" does the "making," the "fathering," and the "humbling"
°**Tells ... corn (line 9):** reveals to me that my hour has come.
°**Zion:** holiest of places.
°**water bead:** water drop, with further suggestion of prayer bead.
°**synagogue:** a place of worship; literally, to bring together.
°**let ... sound:** offer prayers (of mourning).
°**sow ... seed:** shed tears (of mourning).
°**valley of sackcloth:** Sackcloth is worn as a sign of mourning; the phrase recalls the Twenty-third Psalm, a reference consistent with the multiple references to religious themes throughout the poem.

The mankind of her going with a grave truth   15
Nor blaspheme down the stations of the breath°
With any further
Elegy° of innocence and youth.

Deep with the first dead lies London's daughter,
Robed in the long friends,°   20
The grains beyond age,° the dark veins of her mother°
Secret by the unmourning water
Of the riding Thames.
After the first death, there is no other.

Do Not Go Gentle into That Good Night
DYLAN THOMAS (1914–1953)

Do not go gentle into that good night,
Old age should burn and rave at close of day;
Rage, rage against the dying of the light.

Though wise men at their end know dark is right,
Because their words have forked no lightning they   5
Do not go gentle into that good night.

Good men, the last wave by, crying how bright
Their frail deeds might have danced in a green bay,
Rage, rage against the dying of the light.

Wild men who caught and sang the sun in flight,   10
And learn, too late, they grieved it on its way,
Do not go gentle into that good night.

Grave men, near death, who see with blinding sight
Blind eyes could blaze like meteors and be gay,
Rage, rage against the dying of the light.   15

°**stations ... breath:** reference to the Stations of the Cross, depicting the
passion of Christ from trial to Crucifixion.
°**Elegy:** hymn or poem of mourning.   °**Robed ... friends:** buried with all
mankind.   °**grains ... age:** sands of time.   °**her mother:** the earth.

And you, my father, there on the sad height,
Curse, bless, me now with your fierce tears, I pray.
Do not go gentle into that good night.
Rage, rage against the dying of the light.

Which Is My Little Boy
TENNESSEE WILLIAMS (1914–1983)

Which is my little boy, which is he,
Jean qui pleure° *ou Jean qui rit?*°

Jean qui rit is my delicate John,
the one with the Chinese slippers on,

whose hobbyhorse in a single bound   5
carries me back to native ground.

But *Jean qui pleure* is *mysterieux*°
with sorrows older than Naishapur,°

with all of the stars and all of the moons
mirrored in little silver spoons.   10

Which is my little boy, which is he,
Jean qui pleure ou Jean qui rit?

In Westminster Abbey°
JOHN BETJEMAN (1916–1984)

Let me take this other glove off
As the *vox humana*° swells,

°**Jean qui pleure:** John who cries.   °**ou Jean qui rit:** or John who laughs.
°**mysterieux:** full of mystery.   °**Naishapur:** ancient Persian city.
°**Title:** Westminster Abbey in London is the most famous of English cathedrals; it is also the burial place of royalty, statesmen, writers, and so on.
(See lines 5 and 39–40).
°***vox humana:*** literally, "human voice"; a setting of the reeds on a pipe
organ that imitates the human voice.

And the beauteous fields of Eden
   Bask beneath the Abbey bells.
Here, where England's statesmen lie,   5
Listen to a lady's° cry.

Gracious Lord, oh bomb the Germans.
   Spare their women for Thy Sake,
And if that is not too easy
   We will pardon Thy Mistake.   10
But, gracious Lord, whate'er shall be,
Don't let anyone bomb me.

Keep our Empire undismembered
   Guide our Forces by Thy Hand,
Gallant blacks from far Jamaica,   15
   Honduras and Togoland;
Protect them Lord in all their fights,
And, even more, protect the whites.

Think of what our Nation stands for,
   Books from Boots'° and country lanes,   20
Free speech, free passes, class distinction,
   Democracy and proper drains.
Lord, put beneath Thy special care
One-eighty-nine Cadogan Square.°

Although dear Lord I am a sinner,   25
   I have done no major crime;
Now I'll come to Evening Service
   Whensoever I have the time.
So, Lord, reserve for me a crown,
And do not let my shares go down.°   30

°**a lady's:** the speaker's.   °**Boots':** a chain drug store.   °**One-eighty-nine Cadogan Square:** the lady's fashionable address.   °**shares . . . down:** value of her stocks decline.

I will labor for Thy Kingdom,
   Help our lads to win the war,
Send white feathers to the cowards,
   Join the Women's Army Corps,
Then wash the Steps around Thy Throne   35
In the Eternal Safety Zone.

Now I feel a little better,
   What a treat to hear Thy Word,
Where the bones of leading statesmen,
   Have so often been interred.   40
And now, dear Lord, I cannot wait
Because I have a luncheon date.

Hunchback Girl: She Thinks of Heaven

GWENDOLYN BROOKS (1917–   )

My Father, it is surely a blue place
And straight. Right. Regular. Where I shall find
No need for scholarly nonchalance or looks
A little to the left or guards upon the
Heart to halt love that runs without crookedness   5
Along its crooked corridors. My Father,
It is a planned place, surely. Out of coils,
Unscrewed, released, no more to be marvelous,
I shall walk straightly through most proper halls
Proper myself, princess of properness.   10

The Pennycandystore Beyond the El°

LAWRENCE FERLINGHETTI (1919–   )

The pennycandystore beyond the El
is where I first
               fell in love
                        with unreality

°**El** elevated railway.

Jellybeans glowed in the semi-gloom
of that september afternoon
A cat upon the counter moved among
　　　　　　　　　the licorice sticks
　　　　and tootsie rolls
　　and Oh Boy Gum

Outside the leaves were falling as they died

A wind had blown away the sun

A girl ran in
Her hair was rainy
Her breasts were breathless in the little room

Outside the leaves were falling
　　　　　　and they cried
　　　　　　　　Too soon! too soon!

Boy at the Window

RICHARD WILBUR (1921–　　)

Seeing the snowman standing all alone
In dusk and cold is more than he can bear.
The small boy weeps to hear the wind prepare
A night of gnashings and enormous moan.

His tearful sight can hardly reach to where
The pale-faced figure with bitumen eyes°
Returns him such a god-forsaken stare
As outcast Adam gave to Paradise.

The man of snow is, nonetheless, content,
Having no wish to go inside and die.
Still, he is moved to see the youngster cry.

°**bitumen eyes:** eyes made with pieces of coal.

Though frozen water is his element,
He melts enough to drop from one soft eye
A trickle of the purest rain, a tear
For the child at the bright pane surrounded by   15
Such warmth, such light, such love, and so much fear.

To an American Poet Just Dead
RICHARD WILBUR (1921–   )

In the *Boston Sunday Herald* just three lines
Of no-point type° for you who used to sing
The praises of imaginary wines,
And died, or so I'm told, of the real thing.

Also gone, but a lot less forgotten,   5
Are an eminent cut-rate druggist, a lover of Giving,
A lender, and various brokers: gone from this rotten
Taxable world to a higher standard of living.

It is out in the comfy suburbs I read you are dead,
And the soupy summer is settling, full of the yawns   10
Of Sunday fathers loitering late in bed,
And the ssshh of sprays on all the little lawns.

Will the sprays weep wide for you their chaplet tears?
For you will deep-freeze units melt and mourn?
For you will Studebakers shred their gears   15
And sound from each garage a muted horn?

They won't. In summer sunk and stupefied
The suburbs deepen in their sleep of death.
And though they sleep the sounder since you died
It's just as well that now you save your breath.   20

°**no-point type:** Printers measure the size of type in "points."

Church Going

PHILIP LARKIN (1922–   )

Once I am sure there's nothing going on
I step inside, letting the door thud shut.
Another church: matting, seats, and stone,
And little books; sprawlings of flowers, cut
For Sunday, brownish now; some brass and stuff   5
Up at the holy end; the small neat organ;
And a tense, musty, unignorable silence,
Brewed God knows how long. Hatless, I take off
My cycle-clips in awkward reverence,

Move forward, run my hand around the font.   10
From where I stand, the roof looks almost new—
Cleaned or restored? Someone would know: I don't.
Mounting the lectern, I peruse a few
Hectoring° large-scale verses, and pronounce
"Here endeth" much more loudly than I meant.   15
The echoes snigger briefly. Back at the door
I sign the book, donate an Irish sixpence,
Reflect the place was not worth stopping for.

Yet stop I did: in fact I often do,
And always end much at a loss like this,   20
Wondering what to look for; wondering, too,
When churches fall completely out of use
What we shall turn them into, if we shall keep
A few cathedrals chronically on show,
Their parchment, plate and pyx° in locked cases,   25
And let the rest rent-free to rain and sheep.
Shall we avoid them as unlucky places?

Or, after dark, will dubious° women come
To make their children touch a particular stone;

°**Hectoring:** intimidating.
°**pyx:** box in which the Host is carried.   °**dubious:** of doubtful character.

Pick simples° for a cancer; or in some   30
Advised night see walking a dead one?
Power of some sort or other will go on
In games, in riddles, seemingly at random;
But superstition, like belief, must die,
And what remains when disbelief has gone?   35
Grass, weedy pavement, brambles, buttress, sky,

A shape less recognizable each week,
A purpose more obscure. I wonder who
Will be the last, the very last, to seek
This place for what it was: one of the crew   40
That tap and jot and know what rood-lofts° were?
Some ruin-bibber,° randy° for antique,
Or Christmas-addict, counting on a whiff
Of gown-and-bands and organ pipes and myrrh?
Or will he be my representative,   45

Bored, uninformed, knowing the ghostly silt
Dispersed, yet tending to this cross of ground
Through suburb scrub because it held unspilt
So long and equably, what since is found
Only in separation—marriage, and birth,   50
And deaths, and thoughts of these—for whom was built
This special shell? For, though I've no idea
What this accoutered° frowsty° barn is worth,
It pleases me to stand in silence here;

A serious house on serious earth it is,   55
In whose blent° air all our compulsions meet,
Are recognized, and robed as destinies.
And that much never can be obsolete,
Since someone will forever be surprising

°**simples:** plants thought to have medicinal powers.   °**crew . . . lofts:**
people who are experts on the technical details of the structures and uses of
various parts of the church.   °**ruin-bibber:** a bibber is a person who drinks
steadily; a ruin-bibber would get his "kicks" looking at ruins.   °**randy:**
lustful. °**accoutered:** equipped; fitted out. °**frowsty:** musty.
°**blent:** blended.

A hunger in himself to be more serious, 60
And gravitating with it to this ground,
Which, he once heard, was proper to grow wise in,
If only that so many dead lie round.

Unwanted

EDWARD FIELD (1924–   )

I was unwanted then and I'm unwanted now
Ah guess ah'll go up echo mountain and crah.

I wish someone would find my fingerprints somewhere
Maybe on a corpse and say, You're it.

Description: Male, or reasonably so 5
White, but not lily-white and usually deep-red

Thirty-fivish, and looks it lately
Five-feet-nine and one-hundred-thirty pounds:
  no physique

The poster with my picture on it 10
Is hanging on the bulletin board in the Post Office.

I stand by it hoping to be recognized
Posing first full face and then profile

But everybody passes by and I have to admit
The photograph was taken some years ago. 15

Black hair going gray, hairline receding fast
What used to be curly, now fuzzy

Brown eyes starey under beetling brow
Mole on chin, probably will become a wen

It is perfectly obvious that he was not popular at school 20
No good at baseball, and wet his bed.

His aliases tell his history: Dumbell, Good-for-nothing,
Jewboy, Fieldinsky, Skinny, Fierce Face, Greaseball,
     Sissy.

Warning: This man is not dangerous, answers to
     any name
Responds to love, don't call him or he will come.

Underworld

GEORGE GARRETT (1929–   )

You've seen coalminers coming up
for air, all in blackface like
no minstrel show comedian,
but bent over, seamed by the danger
and the darkness they must bear,   5
at once a badge and a wound.

Or maybe a diver on the deck,
his heavy helmet cast aside,
blinking in the hard bright light
where each breath is a gust of fire.   10
It is no laughing matter
to live in two strange worlds.

So it is with certain myths and dreams.
The songs of Orpheus never were the same
after he had seen hell. They roused   15
nothing but rage and madness; yet,
after such vision and total loss,
who wouldn't change his tune?

Oh, you will descend, all right,
dream into the fiery darkness or   20
stumble, awkward among the deep sea
shiftings, troubled by bones
and voiceless cries. And then
you wake and wonder what is real. . . .

Better to come back grinning,   25
scrub the darkness off yourself,
wisecrack with the ordinary seamen,
unless, like a careless saint,
you can give your soul to God.
And then your flesh belongs to furies.   30

The Colossus

SYLVIA PLATH (1932–1963)

I shall never get you put together entirely,
Pieced, glued, and properly jointed.
Mule-bray, pig-grunt and bawdy cackles
Proceed from your great lips.
It's worse than a barnyard.   5

Perhaps you consider yourself an oracle,
Mouthpiece of the dead, or of some god or other.
Thirty years now I have labored
To dredge the silt from your throat.
I am none the wiser.   10

Scaling little ladders with gluepots and pails of lysol
I crawl like an ant in mourning
Over the weedy acres of your brow
To mend the immense skull plates and clear
The bald, white tumuli of your eyes.   15

A blue sky out of the Oresteia
Arches above us. O father, all by yourself
You are pithy and historical as the Roman Forum.
I open my lunch on a hill of black cypress.
Your fluted bones and acanthine° hair are littered   20

°**acanthine:** spiny.

In their old anarchy to the horizon-line.
It would take more than a lightning-stroke
To create such a ruin.
Nights, I squat in the cornucopia
Of your left ear, out of the wind,   25

Counting the red stars and those of plum-color.
The sun rises under the pillar of your tongue.
My hours are married to shadow.
No longer do I listen for the scrape of a keel
On the blank stones of the landing.   30

AUTHOR
AND
TITLE INDEX

(Complete poems and significant portions of long poems only.)